Penguin Books
Tom

John Embling was born in Ballarat in 1952
and grew up in the country near Geelong,
Victoria. He completed an honours degree in
history and philosophy at the University of
Melbourne and worked as a teacher with the
Victorian Education Department, Technical
Division, until 1977 when he resigned.

He now spends his time working with
children from broken homes, and is Director
of the Families in Distress Foundation.

TOM
A child's life regained

John Embling

Penguin Books

Penguin Books Ltd,
487 Maroondah Highway, P.O. Box 257
Ringwood, Victoria, 3134, Australia
Penguin Books Ltd,
Harmondsworth, Middlesex, England
Penguin Books,
625 Madison Avenue, New York, N.Y. 10022, U.S.A.
Penguin Books Canada Ltd,
2801 John Street, Markham, Ontario, Canada
Penguin Books (N.Z.) Ltd,
182-190 Wairau Road, Auckland 10, New Zealand

First published by Penguin Books Australia, 1978
Reprinted 1978, 1979, 1982 (twice)

Copyright © John Embling, 1978
Foreword copyright © Alan Marshall, 1978

Typeset in Baskerville by The Dova Type Shop, Melbourne

Made and printed in Australia at
The Dominion Press, Blackburn, Victoria

All rights reserved. Except under the conditions described in the
Copyright Act 1968 and subsequent amendments, no part of this publication
may be reproduced, stored in a retrieval system, or transmitted in any
form or by any means, electronic, mechanical, photocopying, recording,
or otherwise, without the prior permission of the copyright owner.
Except in the United States of America, this book is sold subject to
the condition that it shall not, by way of trade or otherwise, be lent,
re-sold, hired out, or otherwise circulated without the publisher's
prior consent in any form of binding or cover other than that in which
it is published and without a similar condition including this condition
being imposed on the subsequent purchaser.

CIP

Embling, John, 1952-.
Tom.

ISBN 0 14 004860 x.

1. Adolescent boys – Case studies.
2. Social problems. I. Title.

362.7042

To my mother and father
with love and gratitude

But when time is destroying the present lives of your own children I do not believe that anyone should wait.

Jonathan Kozol

Foreword

This is the story of a typical 13-year-old boy brought up in an environment of industrial city life where the struggle to learn is sometimes hindered by ill-directed teaching, where a longing to be able to read, to write, to understand, is often hindered by staff hampered by inadequate training in the problems arising from the traumatic effect of feeling unloved, not belonging, of being rejected. There are scores of such schools and homes, busy with their subtle task of creating handicaps for the children they produce, man-made handicaps, not those brought about by crippling diseases but by the neglect of parents and the blind refusal of society to face their problems and remove from its laws and rules and regulations those factors that hinder rather than help children reach their full potential.

I had a crippled childhood and was brought up experiencing what I felt was the enmity of people towards my affliction. But I was lucky; I had loving and understanding parents and any resentments I experienced vanished under their faith and belief in me. The children described in this book often lacked this background and their lot was harder.

The author of this book, John Embling, became increasingly aware of the problems facing the children he taught when, as a young teacher in one of Melbourne's outer suburban technical schools, he met the boy who is the subject of this book. He was fortunate in having a fellow worker, a girl called Heather, who had a fine understanding of the underprivileged child's world. So John Embling was able to discuss his problems.

The tragedy of these children is that they rarely

experience a sense of belonging to their parents, to their brothers and sisters, to anyone but misfits like themselves. 'We are all too soft on them,' explained Tom's mother in an attempt to remove responsibility. The children become alienated from their families, rejected by them. They lack a 'caring locality'. Home becomes a coffee shop, a pool room, a pizza parlor: 'The Coffee Shop is an attraction for latchkey kids, the social misfits, the unemployed and the unemployable.' In places like these people such as Heather and John try to reach them and share their lives, a cathartic process involving anguish and trauma on both sides.

During the course of the relationship John Embling found that the learning process was a two way thing. He learnt not only about Tom, but about himself. His feelings and attitudes towards disturbed children were shaped by the best possible means — the experience of working closely with them, sharing their lives and emotions, caring enough to make their problems his own. John sums up this attitude — 'The clinical approach too often ignores that only a caring relationship can help children like Tom Goodwood. I want to understand the child's feelings and reactions and view of things.

'This is what I see as the most promising approach to work with hurt and knotted children: start with the child's basic physicality, concentrating on the initial feelings as they are expressed, then work through the child's blocks and traumas while constantly re-evaluating what is going on. I believe it is important to form a relationship with the child that is honest and physically secure and then to work uncompromisingly through the conflicts. Once the trauma has been located it must be worked on and diffused.'

Throughout the book John Embling shows that words such as 'thief' have a different meaning in Tom's world.

Possessions provide security. 'For Tom it is almost unbearable to part with the pleasure that ownership gives him.' John fills the gap in understanding which often exists between society and its victims, helping us to see Tom's violence, his anger and aggression in a way which all too often reveals our own complicity. Such a book as this exposes the almost inevitable bleakness of the future of children deprived of loving help.

Tom's life is our own seen through a glass darkly.

'Nothing is easier than to denounce the evil villain; nothing is more difficult than to understand him,' wrote Feodor Dostoevsky.

I don't think John tried to teach the children who were his concern. His task as he saw it was to encourage them to teach themselves. There was always a moment when a child discovered within himself a capacity to comprehend. Such a discovery must have been an exciting one. But there were barriers between its translation into knowledge and its death through a lack of that acute sensitivity in the teacher which could have helped the child make it a permanent part of his memory's store.

The life of the average child, however varied his or her upbringing, resembles a walk through a lighted tunnel. He moves from one source of illumination to the next. Sometimes the light flutters and dies and for a time the child is alone in the darkness, then a candle is relit and some light returns. But the light is not very bright and he is given no encouragement from what he sees. A voice is needed, a hand to encourage and lead him, and this is what John Embling supplied. On such a journey it is necessary that his grip be firm, his voice confident, his faith in the outcome of the journey absolute.

What stands out about this particular book compared with other books on emotionally disturbed children is the rare nature of John's own character. He emerges quite unconsciously as a man with a gift of imparting love to those most in need of it, despite rejection and hostility. Working through Tom's problems with him, becoming part of his most intimate adult-child struggle, John reveals much of himself. The development of his relationship with the boy and the growing sense of empathy with him, provide the book with continuity and warmth. Each breakdown in the barrier between them advances their relationship to the stage where John provides Tom's life with a sense of purpose and achievement, converting his initial distrust and hostility into affection. That he was able to do this is a tribute to John's own character, that of a rare and loving human being.

As John became more familiar with the situations Tom was unable to handle he began to understand the reasons for these situations. 'I think I am seeing Tom's problems clearly now,' he says, then goes on to admit that there is still much he doesn't understand.

He talks of the time when first he knew him: 'He was rarely at home, rarely to my knowledge participating in a normal mother-son relationship. Mrs Goodwood cared for her son, he wanted to give out and receive back natural affection, but neither of them knew how to handle their own confused feelings.'

I remember very clearly, as a little boy, returning from school bruised from a fall brought about deliberately by some furious kid kicking one of my crutches from beneath my arm so that I toppled and fell like a tree, looking forward to the comfort of my mother's arms.

Tom had no such escape for his tortured spirit. John gives us a glimpse of his schooling — 'At school, primary and technical, he was hit, abused and humiliated, "they used to hit me almost every day in state school, I got the cuts for anythin' at all . . . at the time me dad left us I got into real trouble with the teachers because I wouldn't do any work. I used to get sent to the office all the time to get the strap . . . almost every day I got it for somethin'. . . me first day at the Tech. Payne gave me six for smokin' and not givin' me cigs to him . . . in me first year there and before I met yuh, I got it for smokin', for not bein' in class, for fightin', for waggin' . . . they used to hit me harder across the finger tips and wrist and I used to get real mad . . . yuh know they'd hit yuh and I'd always go and feel sorry for meself and sit in the toilets each time they hit me . . . I'd sit there all by meself and just get tighter and tighter and I'd wanna kill people . . . I'd hate gettin' in closed rooms after that . . . they'd just beat the hell out of yuh, they knew yuh couldn't do nothin' about it . . .".' I have talked to many children about their most terrifying school experience and it has surprised me the number who remember with terror being in a closed room confronted by a teacher with a strap.

I remember it. But then I am old and situations like that occur no longer. Or do they? If you believe this; if you believe that our children are no longer flogged for misdemeanours, you should read this book written by a unique man, a great man in my book, whose knowledge of children and ability to convey that knowledge to others makes him an outstanding teacher for those reluctant children standing on the edge of the cold sea in front of them, afraid to take the plunge into life, afraid of their inability to swim in its waters, lost amidst strangers on the beach, the society which is supposed to provide them with security.

Alan Marshall

Author's Note

I would like to thank the following people who have contributed to the making of this book: Gwen Dow and Terry Werner; John MacLeod; Lloyd Robson; a friend of many years, Laurie Robson; Jeff Keddie and Stephanie Trigg who helped with typing and read and criticized the successive manuscripts; an American teacher, Marney Wamsley for her kindness in 1976; my family for backing me and a mother who trusted me with her son.

The Literature Board of the Australia Council awarded me a $3,000 General Writing Grant which assisted in the completion of the manuscript.

I wish to thank John Hooker of Penguin Books for creating the opening for this book and Jane Arms and Celia Schmaler who worked sensitively on the editorial process.

Phillip Adams gave active support at a crucial moment.

Special thanks to Heather Pilcher for her encouragement, compassion and insight.

Alan Marshall who has written the foreword to this book has been both friend and adviser; his courage and dignity are an inspiration to me.

A young boy made this book possible in the first place. The book belongs to him and to all the children who taught me more than I was ever taught in school and university.

Introduction

In 1975 I was a young teacher in one of Melbourne's outer suburban technical schools. There I met Tom, a thirteen-year-old on the verge of a complete breakdown. We formed a tentative, yet growing relationship. The diary is the account of our experiences and work together over the next two years. The names have been changed to protect the boy and his family.

The story of Tom is typical of tens of thousands of children in large industrial cities in the western world. The scenes in this book to do with the placing of a ten-year-old in a home for truancy and the infliction of corporal punishment in school are located at specific moments in Tom's past, yet the essence of his life and struggle is universal. Tom's experiences are not exclusive to teachers; they include policemen, social workers, courts, all those involved with youth and institutions, as well as the range of everyday human contact, including his most intimate mother–son, father–son, peer group relationships.

Progressive writers, teachers, psychologists and sociologists have all recorded similar experiences and largely agree upon the basic determinants and preconditions that perpetuate the self-hatred, violence and nihilism of children like Tom. They are: the nightmarish background of child abuse in western society; the growth of cities that are increasingly unfit for sane human existence; the construction of vast, inefficient bureaucracies cut off from the needs of a majority of children and adults; education, welfare and legal systems that are essentially geared to the privileged; teachers, social workers, policemen either insensitive to start with, or made weary and hardened by the sheer inflexibility of their working environment.

Yet the fact remains that children like Tom must be helped to avoid destruction if 'growing up', in the fullest meaning of the words, is to have any relevance to their lives in the post-industrial society of the late twentieth century.

Tom is the story of how one young boy may hopefully have avoided destruction; it is also evidence that for the cruelties and injustices inflicted on our children they still have the courage and spirit to survive.

John Embling
Melbourne, 1978

1975

February

Monday

When I see something for the first time the images remain fixed in my mind. The images I hold of my schools stay with me. Schools are grey. They are made of grey patches. Worn cement paths weave into dull concrete outlines, dull shapes above square, flat boxes. I remember my own schools in this way.

Williamstown Technical School is a building that reflects the era of architectural confusion. It is a mixture of old and new designs, some of which stand out like freckles on a pallid skin. It has old prefabs, a new library, rows of square, concrete trade rooms that run parallel to each other, a hall that is the gym and underneath it, a complex slot-car set-up. As a newcomer I stand back and marvel at its ugliness.

Today I begin my second week of practical experience as a trainee teacher. I am in the remedial English room with fifteen boys who battle with their 'special readers'. They want to read and I find it disquieting listening to them stumble through a page. I am called 'Sir' automatically and when I tell them to call me 'John' they open up with the usual questions: 'Where do yuh come from?' 'Will yuh be takin' us from now on?'

The literacy problem is enormous here and the remedial English section is the real centre of the school. Remedial teaching is of paramount importance, yet even more important is the sensitivity and time needed to understand why these children can't read and write and the implications of that for the rest of their school programme.

The remedial section has only one full-time teacher, Mary Loxley, and two part-time helpers. Mary is harassed by her inadequate working environment and by staff disinterest and hostility towards her work. There seems to me to be something morally disgusting about the staff's refusal to acknowledge and immerse itself in the plight of illiterate, inarticulate deprived children.

This is a disturbing way to start my teaching career. I say this to Mary and she replies, 'There's a hell of a long way from feeling anger to doing anything worthwhile about it. I have lots of boys whose needs make me feel very angry about the system and society. Nobody will help me do anything about it. Many of these boys are constantly slipping out of school and are only capable of minimal concentration when they do roll up. They are often pushy and violent towards students who can cope.' I say that I see very clearly the behaviour and defeatism of boys who are unsure of their place, who feel they don't belong here and who are operating on edgy, explosive feelings most of the time. I tell Mary that I don't want to become just another 'do-gooder' or middle-class teacher who patronises working-class kids. I really want to help these boys survive and live with a sense of their own human dignity.

She looks at me when I say this, probably wondering how long it will be before I take over the Williamstown teaching syndrome which she describes as 'directionless boredom', then says, 'You get on well with a lot of the generally unapproachable boys here. They are friendly and respectful towards you. If you really want to become involved I've got one boy for you to think about.'

She tells me about Tom Goodwood who is soon going to be put into an Institution. He is thirteen years old and comes from a broken home. He occasionally turns up to her remedial English classes. Mary found out that he has a school truancy record. She tried hard to get him to school but found the task was beyond her resources. She says to me, 'I've got half the school to look after, these two small rooms to do it in, and the men on the staff are just waiting to see me fail. What can I really do? I don't have the energy after school to hunt up Tom or to find out what his home problems are. I would hate to see him get locked up. I don't know how he'd survive it. He has been locked up once before and it only made him worse. His mother is a nice person but she can't cope with him. His father left home years ago after constantly beating Tom and his mother, from what I can work out. Tom desperately needs a man to relate to. Will you see if you can do anything with him? He's in so much need of help and I just can't give it to him. I just hope you can get somewhere before it's too late.'

I say, 'Yes, I'll try,' and realize that I have committed myself to something beyond the mere expression of support.

Mary says, 'Thank you. I don't really know what can be done at this stage but I want you to try . . . it means a lot to me. I like him. He's a funny sort of kid.'

Friday

I meet Tom. He is so used to clinical analysis that a detached personal history flows readily forth.

Essentially he is uninterested in talking to me, hanging his head and putting on an appearance of abject boredom. We go for a walk around the block, pick up a couple of orange juices, then sit on the steps of the school hall for about half an hour.

He is a small boy for thirteen; pale, thin, stooped,

stone-faced, with a mop of blond hair. He seems very self-absorbed. Gradually, he starts to open up, 'Me mates, they work at the slaughter yards. They make good money too. Me dad used to work there.'

Tom's father keeps coming up in his conversation and he presents him to me as a sort of hero.

'Me dad shot at the cops. I was with him. They got him. He'd beaten up me mum. He wouldn't go without the cops all fightin' with him. Even then he put up a real blue. He knows all them in the underworld,' says Tom with a swagger.

He was acting out the baby-faced delinquent, exchanging information for orange juice, waiting after each disclosure to see if I wanted to buy more. I suspect him of being more astute than many others realize. Perhaps he identifies with his father's 'career', feeling somehow obliged to act out the criminal image. Most boys want to be in some way like their dad.

I am in Mary's remedial English room after a hectic, overcrowded hour of hearing endless hesitant, stumbling attempts to read. Tom comes in at one stage to see, I think, if I am in, and watches me from a safe distance. Later he reads to me for a few minutes. He reads very slowly without much continuity or understanding, though I have a feeling that this comes more from rustiness than lack of capacity.

Friday night, a week later

Again, as happened last night, a small solitary figure watches me catch the 4.22 p.m. train.

I arrive home late in the evening and look at my bookshelf which is full of words about people and their lives and their ideas. I wonder if there is anything there that will help me make any sense of Tom, Williamstown Technical School and my work there.

I am conscious of some nagging inner feelings and reflect on the boy at the cold railway station. I sense how fragile he must be to need the security of fantasizing his father's heroic shootouts. This is all I see at the moment though I am aware of its limitations.

If I can't ride the crests of his experience, what can I know of his life?

Monday

I see Tom this morning for about ten minutes in remedial English. He is by himself, looking lost, as if he is waiting for somebody. We talk about the football match he saw last Saturday, about the pleasure of riding mini-bikes in summer sand-dunes, and about the boredom of the rest of his life in between. I ask him to read for me, but he says 'I'm not gonna read yuh any of them silly stories.' I think he is quite right in his assessment of them and don't pressure him to read.

Tuesday

I am thinking over the Principal's comments about Tom. He told me he had a short session with the kid towards the end of last year and remarked, 'There's no doubt he's at a crisis stage now. He won't get on with men here. He's just extremely egocentric.' I sat frozen as he said, 'The boy's semi-autistic in a moral sense.' I can see it, the Head in the big chair behind the desk, Tom hunched on the uncomfortable one in front of him, being probed about the difference between good and bad, and right and wrong behaviour. The boy looks up at him from inside his shell, sees the man's lips moving and hears some unconnected words. In that last sentence the Principal compromised his acceptance of Tom.

Wednesday

I take my tape recorder to school today and ask Tom if he wants to use it just for a play around. Tom likes the idea and spends two or three hours recording stuff. These are some extracts from conversations he made with me and one of his friends.

Tom: They don't have dances no more.

Mike: They banned 'em after all the fights.

Tom: Yeah, we used to all go there and pick fights with the sharpies.

John: Where did they come from?

Tom: Footscray. It was no joke, they knocked Lee's head in with an iron bar and his old man went lookin' for 'em and smacked a couple of 'em's faces in.

Mike: Yeah, and the police were all there and everythin'.

Tom: They pick yuh up and shove yuh up in the back seat and give it to yuh with their little brown sticks.

Mike: I'm gonna get the cop who put me in Baltara.

John: How are you going to do that?

Tom: I'll get 'im, yuh'll see.

John: You'd better wait with a large lump of wood on a moonless night in a dark alley. [General laughter]

Tom: And then we used to go after eels in Stan's pond.

John: Did you eat them?

Tom: Yeah, they're real good. Me mum cooks 'em up real nice in batter and yuh put all this sauce and stuff over 'em.

John: I've never tasted eel.

Tom: They're good, yuh have 'em in long pieces.

John: What's the flesh look like?

Tom: Nice, it's all snow white and everythin'. Me mum's a good cook.

Mike: We used to go all the time to Luna Park and have rides on the big dipper.
Tom: That's grouse.
Mike: I used to go on it all the time.
Tom: A lady squashed her baby to death on it.
Mike: Yeah?
Tom: She kept squeezin' it tighter and tighter, and when she got off it was all blue with its eyes stickin' all out.

Mike: Jeez I hate Anderson. He hits yuh all the time for doin' nothin'.
John: Who do you like around here?
Mike/Tom: Nobody.
John: Why not?
Tom: I dunno, it doesn't matter anyway. Yuh can't do anythin' about it.
Mike: I'd like to do somethin' to some of 'em around here.
Tom: Like what?
Mike: I dunno, just somethin'.
Tom: There's nothin' yuh can do. There's nothin' anyone can do.
John: Nothing?
Tom: Except shoot 'em in the head with a shotgun.

Mike: Did yer dad get stuck into yer mum and you?
Tom: Yeah.
Mike: What did he do?
Tom: He'd throw her into walls. One time he was real full, he belted us all and went into the toilet to chuck. He just sat there on the floor and cried.
Mike: What did yuh do then?
Tom: I'd go and kick his head in.
John: Did you?
Tom: Nope.

John: What are you going to do when you leave this place?
Tom: Make money.
John: What about you Mike?
Mike: Make money.
John: Where?
Tom/Mike: The slaughter yards.
John: What are you going to do with it?
Mike: I dunno.
John: Tom?
Tom: How would I know?

Mike: I'm gonna get caught by me mum soon.
John: What for?
Mike: Gettin' out with the boys and these chicks.
Tom: Betty and them mob.
Mike: Jeez they're slack.
Tom: Yeah, they're real moles.
John: But what about you guys?
Tom: What d'yuh mean?
John: Are you any better?
Tom: That's all they're good for. Fuck 'em and leave 'em.
Mike: Yeah, that's what me big brother says. He don't take no cheek from 'em either.
John: Are all your girls like this?
Tom: Yeah, aw, yuh know — not yer sisters and yer mum — aw — not all of 'em anyway.

Tuesday

I think about Tom and me. Where do we go from here? What are my needs in this relationship? Benevolent? Egocentric? Experimental? Unknown? I map out some dangers in my mind. How teacher–student or adult–child orientated is it? I suspect we will be in for a battle and the hardest part will not be our clash of values now, but in time, when we achieve genuine closeness and growing intimacy.

What is my fundamental aim? To try to see the world from Tom's perspective. Ah, that sounds respectable. And what about the need to change his so-called 'anti-social' lifestyle? Will I succumb to pressures to channel his energies in some positive way, whatever that means? I am conscious that in society's eyes teachers are vehicles for producing respectable, 'nice' children.

At present Tom is trying to impress others by playing the tough guy. He is massively unsure of himself and I feel I need to get close to him in little ways, to stop him jamming up physically. He needs to be sure of himself, so that he can relate to people more comfortably and not feel that he has to fight them all the time.

Wednesday

Lisa Golding from Psych. and Guidance comes to see Tom about once every couple of weeks. Today she suggests that I work with Tom and two or three other 'problem boys', to 'socialize them by selective interaction' as she puts it.

Her proposal is that I should 'interact' with him on three levels: formally in the classroom; semi-formally through general student–teacher involvement; and informally through social contact outside the school. She claims that the teaching relationship should aim to 'stimulate his whole personality' and that he needs to 'feel inwardly an order and sequence in his life.' For example, in a reading and writing and taping programme, she suggests that I work on his weaknesses in private tuition, and on his strengths with others in group work to build his self-confidence.

She feels he needs to do things for me, that is, to take

some responsibility and that he needs a lot of oral and verbal work. Perhaps I can tap any interest he has in pop music? I'll give him a few old singles and E.P.s.

The declaration of good intentions sits above me on this page and I merely acknowledge its presence. I prefer to break down walls rather than chip away at them.

Thursday

Tom is not at school. After supervising sport this afternoon, I go to the flats. Tom lives off Koroit Creek Road, on The Strand, Williamstown. It takes half an hour to get there, and I am carrying an achingly heavy bag.

The Strand is a stretch of land along the water's edge, made up mainly of two-storey homes. Williamstown is a curious hotch-potch of the industrial working class — their children, factories, oil supply dumps, high-rise flats, cracked pathways and numerous pubs — side by side with the self-made rich and their lifestyles. The bosses and the bought-in-rich express the workingman's preference for straight, clearcut sexual and community action (based on a strong seaman–convict past), while living themselves in great and expanding material luxury.

It is a clear, warm afternoon. The tug boats, yachts and small fishing craft undulate in a calm sea. The seagulls bathe in the autumn sun, watchful as ever.

I find Tom kicking a football on the sandy patch of lawn before the flats. I leave some records, and ask if he is interested in the remedial English excursion to the zoo tomorrow. He says, 'Yeah'. I saunter back to the station.

The regular contact must be kept going. He disturbs me in a rather elusive way. I am determined to keep cool. I receive another blast from the senior master on how hopeless he is.

'You're just wasting your bloody time. I tried for a while and he just turned bad any time he couldn't get his own way. I've had enough of him.'

I try not to over-blame these people. They spend time and effort on cultivating 'I'm your big mate' or 'You're my little buddy' techniques. They have to give up. When Tom fights off their phoney approaches, they hang on to his rejection to avoid looking into the causes of it. To show Tom you are really for him means patience and a stubborn refusal to be put off by anyone.

Friday

We visit the zoo; Tom seems to enjoy himself.

On our return, I play three games of pool in the deserted staff room with Tom and three others. He is wary still, cautious to get involved in anything of any depth. I think he will try to shrug me off soon, to see if I will stay.

March

Monday

No Tom. After school I go to the flats. The first time I knock, no one is home. The second time, after an amble along the beach, I find his mother, with whom I leave a note. I ask her not to give Tom the impression that there's a hunting party out after a felon when he returns.

I take in the atmosphere of the flats. The Strand is prosperous and spacious. The flats form a mini-island in its midst. I am drawn into a climate that is stuffed with apathy and oppression, feeling the outsider's uncertainty under the gaze of the odd person or couple slouching on the grey balconies, puffing at limp cigarettes, their demeanour matching the grey, grubby, overarching buildings.

Tom's mother, after a few awkward moments, is courteous and open. She was pleased that Tom had talked about school the previous night, and recalled his saying 'At least Mary and John care about me.' This is a reasonable head count. The others view him as an ingrate, not worth their trouble.

I hope the programme can start tomorrow. The implications of his truancy loom, threatening. It would be a mistake to drift on, missing the day-to-day contact. We have to convince Tom, without pressing him too much, of our determination to become involved. Mary told me he once declared, 'All of 'em give up and I see I'm bad anyway.'

Tuesday

At school there is something amiss. Tom is sullen and non-communicative. I feel the 'know not where to go from here' sensation. Yesterday's visit could have set off a reaction at home. I should have known, although it could be something else.

I ignore the sour face and sullen look and ask if he will be around for a while. He answers with a shrug of the shoulders. I guess he'll look in at some lesson and wander off during the morning.

I can't really get a hold on the situation but I do sense that I can't pull Tom in any way without his rejecting me. My theory, as I write this at 9.57 a.m., is that I should be around if I am wanted or if chance makes for a further communication.

I now realize how delicate Tom's make-up is. Having been messed around for years by older people, he has absolutely no trust in people and is mostly withdrawn. My feelings are that I can't get to him: I can't rectify what has happened; I can only act within the confines of what has happened; and I don't know what sets off what. I suspect that just my attempts to get to know him force him to draw away. Nobody seems to know what to do and nobody really seems to care. On that self-indulgent note, I'll go and buy some food at the corner shop.

I feel very vulnerable at times in the school. Being a young outsider in a school dominated by trade teachers, I am unsure of my footing. The power lies not with any particular teacher, but rather with the trade group and its dominant masculinity. The trade teachers feel themselves to be above the average working men. Teaching provides them with the status to rise above the run of the mill working-class blokes. This feeling of superiority makes them often hard and cynical about unhappy working-class boys. The first day I walked into the staff room, a large, overweight trade teacher offered me a seat at his table, then produced a leather strap, whacked in on the table and said, 'You oughta get one of these, son, to keep the little bastards in line with. They don't like it. I once gave three cuts to the whole class of thirty kids, had them holding their hands, bending over, tears running down their faces. Did them a world of good.'

I find it sad that the trade teachers so often refuse to use the mechanical resources which are at hand to work with those boys who shy away from the humanities and science subjects. It seems that to show tenderness to an unhappy child is a sign of weakness. To show it in front of your fellow teachers is to appear unmanly.

There is one man, James Moreland, an ex-R.A.F. pilot, whom I talk to about these things. He can be strong with his boys, yet gentle and sensitive in his bearing. He often says to me, 'John if you can survive here, you can survive anywhere.' I envy him. He can teach mechanics, humanities and ecology and debate the merits of pop music and politics with his classes. When confronted with a potential scene he becomes theatrical and says, 'I'll have your guts for garters', defusing the danger with humour and his own theatrical acting out. I often draw on his strength and experiences when I'm depressed. We have a cup of 'good English tea' and laugh about the absurdities of life. While I draw on Mary's frenetic energy when I feel tired, James's calm helps when I feel disordered and unable to cope.

What a day! I find Tom before lunch in remedial English. He is uncooperative. Mary, full to the back teeth of the staff, their apathy and stupidity, blows up at him. He goes out. I find him with one of his friends, about to go somewhere. We start talking and the cause of his anger comes out.

'I had an argument with me mum about school last night. Yuh told her I wasn't at school.'

That over, he opens up, and after a cigarette we go to the gym to do some exercises.

It is smooth sailing, until I am called away for a few minutes.

When I return all the kids are lined up round the walls. The Egyptian gym instructor is strutting about, screeching in some incomprehensible dialect, pushing Tom and four others into his office. He pulls out his strap, shouting, 'You no play here without teacher, you no come here by self, you no . . !'

I start to say, 'I think you've made a mistake, I had to go for . . .' but he takes off again.

'They no come here by self!'

'Excuse me, but I was merely called away.'

He breaks in. 'All right, I fix this up and we talk then,' waving his strap about.

I have no choice. 'Tom's with me, get the idea, good! Come on, let's go.'

The Egyptian stares, eyes popping, and I'm getting hot in the face.

Outside Tom observes, 'He's a suck.'

I couldn't allow the confrontation to go on. I never was a non-interventionist, or hid behind professional ethics. The man was a bully, refusing to let the boys explain my brief absence.

We go into town after lunch to shrug off the morning mood, eat some pancakes and talk about bikes and cars. Tom returns by himself, amiable and relaxed.

I agree with the view that you must be on the disturbed child's side, not as a protective blanket, but as a real support in stressful moments. It is worth the effort.

April

Thursday

Tom comes in by 10.30 a.m. in good humour. We go to the library. He is still drawing long, shiny-bladed knives, page after page of them. He now looks me in the face.

Mary is helping to construct a limited timetable for Tom that will use sympathetic teachers and develop the basic literacy and numeracy skills. This is a highly selective process.

In the afternoon, between my fourth forms, Tom and I have a long session. He begins to sketch facial outlines, images of skinheads with tattoos, earrings, huge eyes and teeth and scarious complexions. They are all mean and tough. We talk about learning. I feel he wants to learn, yet forces himself to say, 'I know 'nuff for me.' He can barely form the letters of his own name; he looks and feels vulnerable when he is writing.

He plays on the gym trampoline, then we have a

couple of games of pool on the staff table. He takes the tape recorder home for the weekend.

This is an extract from a tape he made alone. His voice is clear and articulate, his manner slow and relaxed.

'I like music because it's just a good feelin'. Some kids like it just because their mates like it; I don't. I like it as it gives me a real good feelin', and it makes me, yuh know, just wanna dance. Sometimes I dance, but not much, not around people, I think they're gonna laugh at me or somethin', it's not funny.'

Saturday night

Tom belongs in no clear cut diagnostic category. Too many disturbing things have coincided in his life depriving him of normal childhood experiences: family violence, the loss of his father, institutionalization for being 'in moral danger', years of truancy and clashes at school. It will be hard for him to cope with society's demands as he gets older. He senses the generally accepted norms of behaviour and that his actions are somehow different. This makes him vulnerable to adult violence and fearful of rejection. Society remains outside his experiences. Its values are only incorporated in his life in disjointed fragments and an achingly painful awareness exists of his separateness. 'What's so good about anythin' anyway?' he often says, 'I can get by all right by meself.'

Monday

I sit talking to the kids as they work on various things. I have a feeling of well-being on this warm, windy morning. Tom is here too, pottering around, amiable and relaxed. In the back of my mind I see him mooning around a group for longer than usual. I sense something is building up there, and slowly ease around in the chair, making some crack to distract him. He wanders off, playfully clipping someone on the ear. I'm about to make some remark and the kid pushes him away. Okay, I think, that's settled. Then he goes wild, smacking the kid in the face. I leap up and am moving towards him as he picks up a chair. A sea of blank faces turns to see what I am going to do. As he lifts the chair above his head I grab him as he screams, 'Fuck off, I wanna kill 'im,' tears of anger running down his face. The kids are watching, intent on the struggle. He is rigid with rage, making it hard for me to pin his wrists together. The chair falls away, leaving us both wrestling in the centre of the classroom. The screaming goes on and on, louder and louder, 'I'm gonna kill 'im, I'm gonna kill 'im,' as I carry him writhing and squirming from the room and down the passage shrieking and fighting wildly. Teachers and students stare out at the noise. I head for the gym locker room with Tom kicking at the doors that shoot past. Nearly there. I have to wrench him off the door handle. Inside, I let him down. He comes at me, charging, kicking and screaming, 'Get outa me way!' I pin him hard against the wall, aware of my aching limbs. When he relaxes against the tension, I let him break away, and he picks up the pole for opening the high windows.

The Vice-Principal enters, takes in the scene, and says, 'Are you all right?'

'Fine', I answer.

He says, 'Mrs Goodwood's here at a parent meeting. I'll go and get her. Can you hold on for a while?'

'Sure.'

He departs, and Tom paces around with the pole, jerking it about with growing agitation. Gnawing inside me is an awareness of looming, outside forces. A line from a book goes around in my head, about if one has to go mad, the tactic to learn in our society is one of discretion.

Crash! A pane of glass breaks. The pole goes up in the air and crashes through another. Glass is sprinkled, glistening on the floor. I seem to half-realize it all from another world, distant from what is going on.

Tom picks up one of the larger, jagged edges, yelling, 'I'll cut youse all up, get outa me way! I'm gonna kill 'im.'

The word discretion comes to mind again, and I focus on the sparkling piece of glass. I try to reason with him, but to no avail.

He's up close now, the glass in his hand, waving it up and around.

'I'm not moving Tom so you may as well attack me with it or put it down.'

He shrieks at me, 'Fuck up!' and the glass splinters against a wall. I try to calm him down, telling myself I can't let him out until he cools off. He screams something inarticulate, charging against me, then into the walls, smashing a mirror and some light globes.

I sense the battle may be lost, yet refuse to face the consequences, so I make another attempt to get inside him.

He is yelling repeatedly about killing people; that nobody cares about him; to leave him alone; that he doesn't need anybody; and over and over, 'Let me out, let me out!' His face is all puffed up, livid with rage, years of betrayal and guilt pouring out.

I try to reach him again with humour, anything I can think of. At certain moments he twists himself in a ball and there's an explosion of sound before he whirls his body in the walls and windows.

'Let me out, let me out!' He crashes into me. My body hurts. He can't go out, it will be back to the Home, and more confinement. The only thing to do is to wait and let the frustration come out and then subside. Something is not being touched deep down inside him, he is carrying something within him that can't stand the world. And I don't give a damn for operant conditioning, Freudian psychoanalysis, or the classification of human behaviour. All I care about is the pain confronting me, the screaming knot of a person clearly communicating his helplessness. This is his way of striking out for some measure of self-worth, to show the world that he can't express himself in any other way. The message is loud and clear.

'Look at what I am and what is bottled up inside me!'

Of course this isn't the end of the line. To some it would have been. In other circumstances the consequences may have been catastrophic. In many ways, it is the beginning of Tom's self-realization. The scene represented a display, heightened by some build-up from the previous days, of what Tom feels he cannot live with. He was set off by physical intervention, reacted to the 'audience' observing him, and had no inner means of coping with the confinement I placed around him. He feels his world is a prison. The adults in it are callous warders, he can find no security in social interactions and he has no self-esteem. Most of all, Tom expressed his need to relate to another person. He wanted what George Dennison calls the 'reality of encounter' with another human being. When his tantrum failed to provoke the expected reaction he was left with his own image in the mirror. Shortly after the scene he grew quiet. For a day or more he was shy, then apologetic. He didn't want to lose one of his few reference points, or areas of regular human contact. The outburst was a healthy sign. In another context it may have been misinterpreted and the pain expressed merely reinforced.

Sunday

I take him to the coast for the day. We climb and crawl up the Point Addis cliffs in a sunny, breezy atmosphere with few people around. I want to let him begin to feel at one with nature. A full tide surges its frothy foam on the soft sands. Our nostrils and lungs take in the fresh air as we watch the distant board-riders shooting timelessly across the waves. The panorama from the cliff-tops is quite staggering. It almost induces dizziness. Tom is animated, running and jumping among the rocks on the shore, searching through the rock-pools, spraying water as we play together. He is reluctant to leave, and becomes quiet and withdrawn as we near Williamstown in the fading light of the dusk.

We find his mother and sister watching T.V. Tom goes in, armed with the deserted fishing cage full of seaweed and rusty wire that we found. I depart, feeling empty and sad at the incomplete family I have left behind.

'You can't combat the home background,' they say.

Tom doesn't want too many strangers calling in to inspect him. Once he told me, 'It makes me feel somethin' must be wrong with me, with them just starin' right at me, askin' me all these things. I get real sick of it.'

Monday

Mary, Lisa and I have a quiet morning coffee together. Both Mary and Lisa are strong, caring women in a school dominated by a feeling of hostile masculinity. Mary is seen as a fussy over-protective mother by the majority of the men in the school, 'She just wants to mother all the boys and lets them get away with too much,' one trade teacher told me after she had confronted him over the strapping of one of her slow learners. She was red with anger and when I saw the boy's swollen hand and arm I felt the same myself. Every now and then one of her boys is singled out for rough treatment. The men draw back from her direct manner and I suspect they are wary of her hot temper.

Lisa comes to the school once a week to see Tom. She has courage and is unafraid of the chauvinistic atmosphere that greets her at staff meetings.

I wonder if these women will last in their work. Lisa is a psychologist without power in the schools she visits. She is only here on 'referral' which may be terminated at any time. How is she to keep the trust of an already suspicious child when she has no actual supportive power?

Mary and Lisa must work in environments that are unresponsive to their warmth and dedication. I hope they have the inner sustenance to fight on.

Tuesday

Mary tells Lisa and me about yesterday's staff meeting. The staff had voted to clamp down and force Tom to go to classes.'How,' I ask, 'do you force a truant back to school activities?' I feel so frustrated it is unbelievable.

The boy wanders happily about the school, feeling it out for the first time. I go to see the Principal, who is also unaware of yesterday's gathering. He aligns himself with my approach, though possibly only because he hadn't been informed about what was going on.

'I want to know about any meeting held in this school.' He goes on to recollect a moment last year when Tom went rigid and Lisa had to be called in. She had sat on the floor with him to get him to talk. What else had taken place, I wonder. I distrust the Principal's explanation here. Perhaps the Principal was frightened by the sheer intensity of the boy's behaviour and didn't want to provoke something that he couldn't handle. He added, 'I get the feeling that one of these days something will go snap in him.'

Tuesday, a week later

I take Tom with a group to see *The Towering Inferno*. He is becoming healthier, less strained and drawn in the face, and not as shrunken and hunched as before. He likes the film, the crumbling building and human chaos within it. His favourite film is *Earthquake*, another disaster film epic, full of noise and bodies and mess.

I notice during the film interval that he can't read the names of the refreshments; he works by sight and past experience.

I am still convinced of staff animosity towards our work with Tom. The reading campaign is very slow. I have given him some comics, a printing set, some paints and a book of riddles to work with.

Sometimes I feel as though I am walking through a therapeutic zoo, full of captions and stuffed replicas of the ideal person. 'This person has actualized', 'here is reformed man', 'this was once a deviant child'. Walking through the labels, forms and types, only a conglomeration remains.

May

Monday

There are two others besides Tom in the group now. Peter, fourteen, is a very hostile boy and conscious of his developing physical prowess, he is able to stop the staff imposing any corporal punishment on him. Tony is younger, clever, undersized and quick-tongued. His father died last year leaving a strained, weak mother to bring up her son.

Tom has a great need to act up in front of them, though right now he seems anxious to share work opportunities with others like himself. He wants group involvement.

They paint, draw, sing and listen to themselves on the tape recorder. I leave them alone, aware of the free-flowing interactions. All three have 'records' for truanting and theft. As I watch, talk with and teach them, I feel the inequality and bloody-mindedness of the legal system as it is applied to working-class kids.

Tom spent six months in an Institution for truancy and for 'being in moral danger'. An awful alienation stays with him. Mrs Goodwood tells me, 'Tom wouldn't talk to me for the first few weeks, he just kept crying when I went to see him. He screamed and kicked when they took him away.' The phobia of people deserting him made him feel alienated from himself and his family and life's potential. He must have felt unbearably alone, lost, powerless in captivity. His mother found a changed, tense, distrusting boy when he was allowed to go home.

She tells me there has been a change in his behaviour in the last few weeks. 'He comes home early, and even talks about school things. He never used to do that.' I tell her to expect moments of tension and frustration as he tries out new things and feels his relationship with the world.

Today, one of the teachers who previously said Tom needed a good kick in the behind, asks about his background, and says, 'If I'd known why he didn't relate well to standover tactics, I'd have been more careful.'

Friday

I chat to Lisa about Tom's past. It dawns upon me: he was in the Institution nearly three years ago. From my conversations with Tom it seems barely yesterday, a nightmare of intimate reality.

Lisa is pleased with our progress; she suggests I write up what has happened in relation to the past problems to show how things are evolving, hopefully, for the better.

At the end of Term I, Tom comes regularly to school. His moods still vary enormously as he looks for a place to grow up in, to catch his self-esteem in balance. For whatever reason, I am moved by his efforts and have tried to do my best for him over the past few weeks.

June

Monday, first day, second term

Tom, Peter and Tony take me on a guided tour of their bike tracks, hollow trees, playgrounds and secret places. Back at school we play roulette. Tom interrupts it momentarily when he is losing and quits, trying to upturn the table. The others tell him, 'Fuck off, if yuh're not gonna play proper.' He mopishly stays around, watching the game.

Tuesday

We go on a school trip to the slaughter yards and I recall the dark reds and blacks of Dante's *Inferno*. It leaves me with images of slashed throats and rows of gutted carcasses. I'll never forget the buckets of blood, the endless tunnel of workers in messy overalls, and the frothy mixture of red ooze and soapy detergent on the floor.

The kids lap it up, the cavernous world and all its mush. I order a salad sandwich for lunch, minus the usual slice of ham, much to their delight. We have a look at the Williamstown cemetery on the way back. Tom, Peter and Tony were greatly attracted to the built-in imagery in their own reactions. Their imaginations are fired by the overgrown and submerged parts of the graveyard. Tom is fully animated and, eyes ablaze, recounts thrilling tales of mystery and horror.

I am still bothered by the insensitivity of Tom, and of the other two to a lesser extent, to the friction points of the world around them. He drifts on, largely oblivious to the range of human temperament about him.

That night I dream of teachers in blood-spattered aprons, armed with hatchets, with kids suspended from trolley hooks . . .

Thursday

Today's account is an example of our daily hassles. Lisa arrives with Tom, concerned about a confrontation Tom had with Payne yesterday afternoon. I had let the three of them out at 2.15 p.m. (school ends at 2.30), and some teacher grabbed them for 'loitering around the bike sheds', according to Tom, and took them to Payne. He had carried on for a while about school rules, and said he'd see them at lunchtime tomorrow.

We are concerned that petty enforcements are undermining Tom's gradual integration into school activities. Mary Loxley says that Payne is a standover type, putting forward one face for the Psych. and Guidance crowd, and his more usual face for the rest.

He was demanding to know why Tom hadn't been to his regular classes. Lisa and I have a long talk to the Vice-Principal and he convenes a staff meeting for next Wednesday morning to let everyone know what's going on.

Lisa is still pleased with our progress. She fears that other teachers, those lacking sympathy, can subvert the improvements made.

All three boys were late for school today, tense and

worried about yesterday's run-in. We have a heavy cathartic session with the gym punching bag.

Wednesday

We have a morning staff conference. Lisa and I present what has been achieved with Tom and we discuss our aims and how we hope to progress. I feel frustrated and angry, as just before the meeting, Payne and another teacher told me they would have to take strong action about an incident on a train yesterday, when Tony had said 'fuck' to the others, and a passenger had a fit and rang the school to complain.

'We can't have these kids making a fool of us,' Payne said. Luckily the Principal intervened and amicably settled the matter.

Friday

After a number of good sessions, Tom has a clash with Mary in remedial English, ripping up his timetable and declaring, 'I'm not comin' here no more.' I see him later in the gym with the others. After a short play around with them, I say I have to go, to which they reply, 'We ain't comin' here no more, or to school at all.' I shrug my shoulders, saying something about all the free time I'm going to have to myself. Mary is quite sure they will head off after that rebuff, however after a while they come to find me, trying to reconcile their pride and slight annoyance. We troop off for a game of pool after school; another drama ends.

July

Monday

Tom's mother is waiting at the school gate. He hasn't

been home for three days. I find Tony and Peter, and they think he might be at Bill's in Newport. We check this out and find, in a diseased dwelling with six or seven other young kids, among rotten baked-bean tins, beer bottles, half-smoked cigarettes and dirty mattresses on the floor, hidden in a sunless corner, the dirtiest, filthiest, palest Tom imaginable. I have forgotten to mention the cats which were ambling in the rubbish; mangy bruised creatures, racing off at our entrance. Tom looks straight through us, smothered in the grimy, dingy atmosphere. I can see his eyes and hollow, blank expression, I smell the stench and putridness, and feel the distrust and awkwardness when I enter.

His mother is deeply shocked and on the verge of tears. She goes home. I stay. The boys are all friendly and responsive once approached as individuals with their own needs and interests recognized. We spend most of the day yarning about things. Then Tom goes off home.

The pertinent facts as I see them now are that the school administration is prone to push the panic button at any new development in Tom's lifestyle; that his mother is finding him more and more unreachable; that the child is searching for his identity, living under an acute sense of disharmony with the world around him, going from one activity or group to another; and that we aren't really sure what his problems are in a casual sense, that is, what's wrong with him right now.

There is something terribly ajar in his makeup. I am unable to understand why he acts as he does. I can see the patterns of his behaviour but I can't penetrate the exterior shell and grasp his motivation. His presentation is so variable, a charade for a series of split forces; overlapping character needs fermenting inside him. I can reach him to a point; beyond that the territorial defences seem impregnable.

Wednesday

I think Tom needs an environment in which he can act out his 'delinquency' and then catch up on his lost development, the years in which he has been riveted to the traumas of the family breakup. He has come to the teenage years of conflict and transition ill-equipped to accommodate the turmoils involved. Fear of punishment, and the sort of humiliation imposed on him at school both exaggerate the emotional manifestations of what his past environment has done to him. A simple reward–punishment approach would be torture.

Friday

We play pool. He loses, getting progressively more bad tempered. 'Why should I always lose?' I play on, ignoring his antics, until he gets over this bad temper. I unobtrusively allow him to catch up and win, attempting to concentrate the fire within him in a self-nourishing direction.

He cannot accept that his father rejected him and walked out on him. His father's desertion of his mother and the family is of secondary importance.

How does an eight-year-old boy understand desertion? How can he compensate for his loss? What are his compensatory mechanisms? Tom's reaction has been to think he is responsible for the desertion. He must have caused it. Therefore he is bad, he is guilty. How can he live on with this guilt and remain sane?

Tom projects his guilt on to other people. His mother must be responsible. She caused his father to leave. He projects this problem on to everyone he meets. He doesn't trust anyone. They will all let him down. He thinks they all expect something of him, which leaves him open and vulnerable to their actions. He will never let any man or father-figure close enough to hurt him.

By projecting these feelings on to other people, he restricts the quality of any later relationships, punishing himself in the process. He inflicts the form of the father–son relationship on every human contact, disallowing the possibility of his participation in any fuller, more satisfying way. He pays all his life for the confusion over the responsibility for his father's desertion.

Saturday

It's not just an analytical experience for me that demands neat explanations. I want to change the direction of his life-flow, to help him stand out against all the forces and currents that will be the seeds of his destruction. I don't want to act against his trust. I want an immediate grasp of reality.

What does he want and need?

August

Saturday

I have started to work with four or five older friends in Tom's peer group. We play pool, have a few beers, talk about the problems of everyday life that confront them.

Lee is sixteen. He is the peer group leader. Old ladies like him. He carries an élitist air, almost debonaire. Lee looks after the younger boys and protects them from the outside world, as well as from the peer group itself. His control is remote. He doesn't manipulate from within the normal peer group structures. The method he uses is more that of the intelligence agent. He gleans information from local resources — admiring girls, shopkeepers, mothers and railway station workers. Lee has a subtle way of drawing out information from people. As I get to know him better, he takes me further into his world.

Drew is Lee's side-kick, more withdrawn, but with an explosive personality. There are many scenes of violence in his past. They lie just below the surface ready to erupt at the slightest intrusion into his being. The boy also suffers from intense claustrophobia. One day he told me, 'Me mum locked me in the toilet once, took the slats out of the air vent and pelted me with beer bottles.'

While Lee is a fist fighter, the exponent of the knock-out punch, Drew is extremely vicious with his feet. Lee is of medium height with a compact build. Drew is like a panther who slinks up on his prey. With a mixture of beers and port inside him, he is capable of almost anything. Initially I was unaware of his continual presence around me. His needs are great and I am hesitant at times with him.

Jim is the outsider in this group. He is Tom's age, a most reticent character. He will tell me about the Bible and its stories. Extremely perceptive in human relationships, he has lived largely in the world of the mystic. His mother runs the local spiritualist church. Jim has a crying need for a strong father-figure. His own father died when he was very young. My relationship with him tends to be in terms of this need.

I am spending a few weekends in their company around the bike tracks, beaches and drive-ins.

Sunday

From what I can construct from conversations with his mother, grandmother, Mary Loxley and Lisa Golding in particular, Tom's upbringing was centred around a break-down in his parents' relationship. He has had most to do with women; his mother and grandmother have provided the only stability and love in his life. His mother says, 'He was real good in the early years. At home and even when he was at school, he got on good with everybody until his father left. He was about eight then, and he began to truant from school and never tell us anything. He started to lie to me about what he was going to do, and lie to them at school, saying things like I wouldn't let him go to school and I was hitting him at home. And he wouldn't make friends with anyone, he'd just hang around with one group for a while and then go somewhere else.'

I don't know what broke the family up. From what I can make out, Tom's father came and went at regular intervals, until his mother decided to terminate the marriage. She says of his relationship with Tom, 'He'd be real good sometimes, taking Tom out fishing, and all of us to picnics and the footy. He'd be real kind, and buy us things. Then he'd just ignore the boy, even when he told him he'd take him out somewhere. Tom couldn't understand, and Jim would get angry with him and yell and shout and knock him out of the way. He just turned on and off. Sometimes he'd come home drunk and we'd fight, then he'd be sorry and try to make it up to us all. I'm worried Tom will be the same. Some mornings he gets up in a good mood, then others he won't get up at all and won't talk to me. I never know where he's going. Sometimes he goes up to mum's or the hospital where she works and asks for money, or stays the night with her. Sometimes he comes in with boys I've never seen before.'

His mother's real fear is that her son will turn out like his father. This underlying fear can be partly self-fulfilling. The son introjects his mother's concern; it becomes part of his growing self and is projected back on to his mother and increases her mounting fears. Yet her doubts are grounded in everyday observations. She said to me once, 'Perhaps there was something wrong with my husband that has been carried on in Tom.' I doubt this very strongly, yet the notion of some genetic malfunction persists in her mind and affects her relationship with him. He lives with this cloud over him, reinforced by experiences of institutionalization and school failure.

September

Tuesday night

The time has come to sort through my own needs as I work with Tom and others.

I come from a lower middle-class background. My high school education was in a traditional public school. I dropped out of a law course in 1971 over Vietnam and my refusal to register for conscription. An honours degree in history and philosophy led me nowhere. I was searching for some depth and meaning in my life. The university world seemed terribly impersonal. People walked around wearing masks of radical politics, masks of aesthetic soulfulness. I never found human warmth there.

Not fitting into any specialist box of academic knowledge, I drifted along my own interest grooves. The writings of committed psychologists, anthropologists, novelists took hold of my imagination.

A feeling of dissatisfaction haunted me. I decided to enrol as a student teacher. I wanted to contribute something to the everyday struggles of mankind. Crouched over a small desk at a university doing 'research' was not for me. I wanted to be in what George Dennison calls 'the real lives of children'.

Wednesday night

Williamstown Technical School is a working-class school caught in the consequences of an educational transformation. A few years ago, a progressive Principal attempted to change a traditional suppressive technical school into an open, cooperative one. He brought about a sharp facelift, abolishing school parades and compulsory uniforms, limiting corporal punishment, initiating a programme of open units and school activities alongside the formal classroom teaching. After a series of internal battles he left and a new structure was imposed upon the school. Time eroded the edifice, leaving a framework of liberal education run by people largely uncommitted to its survival. The school is presently in limbo, drifting if anything, in a conservative direction.

Tom came to Williamstown Tech. in 1974, with a primary school record of truancy and misbehaviour. The school's atmosphere was not conducive to the needs of a kid designated as a 'problem child'. He was known to be extremely retarded in reading, writing and mathematics, socially immature, and incapable of coping with the male staff — the majority. From the teachers' point of view, he had been inadequately socialized. Mrs Goodwood remembered the times he got the strap for truanting.

His school life is largely unpredictable and irregular. Personal contacts are unreliable and unrewarding in the school setting; inevitably he truants, wandering about, building up an intimate world of things, of places where he can hide. The fishing spots, the familiar trees, the bike tracks, even the horse yards he likes so much, are dependable and predictable. However, by seeking an identity away from the school environment, he fails to assimilate the fixed ways of gaining social acceptance; he remains 'outside', liable to social ostracism. In fact, my analysis of his situation in these terms assumes a tacit acceptance of the prevailing political and moral attitudes to these children.

October

Monday morning

Tom and the group haven't arrived yet. I am thinking over the weekend activities. We attended a camp just out of Melbourne with a group from the local community centre. Rosemary Heathcote, the youth coordinator, invited me to bring along Tom and a couple of other boys I knew. We left on Friday night, met a group from another community centre in the western suburbs of Melbourne, and headed off for the three nights and two days which turned out to be sheer hell. The organization had been worked out between Rosemary and the youth leader of the other group. How can I describe him? The second Messiah himself, wearing a silver cross on his large black football hat, beaming with benevolence on all around him. 'Bless you, my son,' he said as he introduced himself.

The campsite was an old Japanese prisoner of war camp: nothing had been done to it since. A lake full of reeds and snags lay opposite it. Kayaks and mini-bikes were available for use. To take thirty kids who are neither used to the freedom of the country, nor to kayaks and mini-bikes, was far from wise; on top of that taking rival gangs from different suburbs was bloody stupid. The 'Messiah's' group, contrary to previous agreements, started to consume large quantities of alcohol which they had brought with them. Our gang, not to be outdone, walked the ten kilometres to the nearest pub, and returned with a huge amount of the amber liquid. To be fair they did bring back some cans for Rosemary and me.

Rosemary was extremely agitated with the situation. As she put it, 'God help us now; it only takes two beers to send them 'loco'. If I get my hands on the person responsible for this there may be a second crucifixion.'

What am I doing here, I wondered. There was pandemonium all around me; a boy in a drunken stupor slipped off his stool into the fire; another kept stripping off in public to be the centre of attraction. Mini-bikes roared incessantly, drunken kids went rowing on the lake on a pitch-dark night; a girl was found hopping from bed to bed 'consoling' the drunken youths. One boy had an accident which partly severed his finger. When he discovered it was a half-hour trip to the nearest hospital he decided to stick it back with a band-aid.

Meanwhile, some volunteers tried to arrange a prayer meeting, Rosemary washed dishes, repaired damages and rescued the drunks from the lake. I had a flour bomb tossed through my window by a rather drunk kid and got splinters of glass in my arm. Some camp!

My thoughts are interrupted by the arrival of Tom and the group.

'How's yer arm, John? Jeez it was the best camp we've ever had!'

Wednesday
My teacher-training supervisors, Joy Banks and William Turner, are cautious about my growing involvement with Tom and other unhappy boys at Williamstown Tech. Joy runs the university's most

innovative teaching-training course. She is a committed socialist who believes in the importance of working-class children receiving a serious, solid education. William is an experimental psychologist. He is an open-minded, friendly man. We get on well.

I am grateful to Joy for the work she has done to establish the course. It has a very flexible structure that allows the students to follow up their own interests. Joy told me at the start of the year something that has stuck with me. She said, 'It is always an honour to be taken into the world of a hurt child. When a child learns to trust an adult again, the trust must be respected.'

I think Joy and William are uncertain as to where my work with Tom will lead.

November

Friday night

We go to a pop concert. Tom has been excited for weeks about it, telling other kids, 'I'm really gonna see Sweet at Festival Hall.' He regulated his behaviour so as not to offend anyone, 'just in case I won't be able to go.'

At the concert he becomes restless, disturbed by the sheer impersonality of the crowd and the overwhelming noise. After an hour or so, he looks positively ill, so we leave. Back to Williamstown, he feels well again. The expectations of the past weeks have been forgotten, as if they never existed. We do something else. No activity can hold his interest for long, he can't seem to allow it any prolonged concern. How can I reach him while this restless, erratic turmoil reigns?

On another level there is a total incapacity to cope with doctors or dentists or anything involving close physical contact. Every imposition becomes a terrifying threat to his existence. Like a frightened, concerned animal on the defensive, in a blind panic, he lashes out at the closest intruding object.

December

Saturday

I want to explore the inner world of Tom Goodwood using what I have gleaned from our relationships and experiences together so far. What is his inner world really like in the ordinary, everyday ways?

I try to grasp what must go through Tom's mind and reflect on four of his typical experiences.

The morning is cold. He sleeps on, weary from the night before, shutting out the noise of people and cars in the street. Then he feels a cold moist hand against his face; angrily brushes it away.

'It's time to get up Tom, your breakfast's ready.'

His aching body, fighting away the light and sound of day, falls into the dark corridors of sleep. His mother opens the blinds, shakes him by his turned-away shoulder, 'Now come on Tom, get up, don't be a nuisance.'

Blinding annoyance. 'Go away will yuh.'

The mother goes out, leaving him awake and irritable 'Why don't yuh fuck off' races around his mind.

He tries to go back to sleep. The memory banks are coming awake, the images of the night before flood into consciousness.

'Now come on, your breakfast will get cold, it's nearly twelve o'clock.'

He tosses from side to side, suddenly jumping up, pulling the bed apart, sending a lamp flying.

'Now don't be silly Tom, you're always in a bad mood

when you come in so late, and you promised you'd be home earlier after the last . . .' He brushes angrily past her into the bathroom.

She watches him glued to the T.V., watching 'them silly cartoons' all the time, wondering what he might have done last night. She feels a mixture of concern and tiredness. 'Here I am, unable to sleep, with him out, expecting me to wait up to whatever time he comes in. I'm on these tablets and I've never been like that, and he just comes and goes as he pleases.'

The sullen face, small hunched body, crouches in front of the set, half a crumpet left on the plate near his feet.

'I don't know, perhaps I'm to blame. No, that's silly, his father's in him, that's the problem.' Her thoughts run, jumping from one mood to another, as she washes the dishes sparkling clean.

He sits, enthralled in the animated figures, watching their movements, the world ordered in their action. Nothing gets in, his perception complete in the story he can feel and understand. His mother becomes agitated, unable to recognize the simple unity of the boy in his fantasy world.

She interrupts, 'Are you coming to the footy with us?' No reply.

'Now Tom, are you listening to me?' Nothing. She picks up the plate, knocking it against his leg. He reacts.

'What do you want?'

'Are you coming to the footy with us?'

'No.'

'You never come as you used to. Don't you want to be seen with your mother any more?' A shrug.

'Leave me alone will yuh.'

'Well, where are you going? You're not going out riding with Lee.' He grits his teeth, picks up a pillow and sends it into a wall.

'Leave me alone will yuh.'
She walks, beaten, into the kitchen.

It's a windy, overcoat afternoon and Tom and his mates are in a deserted swampy tip which is covered in black briquette dust; the chill atmosphere is pierced by the muffled, spluttering, roaring sounds of bikes in motion. He feels content, enclosed in this island of noise and action, perched on top of the brown rusted remains of a '64 Holden, cigarette in one hand, beer can in the other. The bikes shoot in and out of view, angling the narrow pot-holed corners, speeding down the long bending stretch, slowing into the hazardous jump, jerking airborne over it and sliding to a halt short of the barbed-wire fence. Tom feels full of vigorous animation, and yells at Lee, 'Come on, it's my go.'

'Wait until yuh've finished yer beer.'

'Nuh, I'm right now.' Beer in hand, he jumps on the clutch, the motor roars out, propelling the bike upwards and forward.

'For Christ's sake, watch the bloody clutch will yuh'. The bike veers from side to side, barely avoiding a large rotten stump on the track, hitting a pool of mud and water, spraying it back in his face. The beer can falls, rolling away into the bushes. Lee and Tony stand watching. 'He's bloody mad that guy. He'll kill himself one of these days.'

'Yeah, when he drinks he drives like an idiot.' They climb up on the skeleton car to follow his course.

'I feel great, shouldn't have dropped the beer though,' Tom reasons, the wind whistling in his head, the world rising, falling as he kicks the ground shooting by and presses the throttle tighter, the motor shaking and straining with the effort. The bike shoots carelessly along the twisting, slippery track. The boys watch silently from the car roof, their hearts beating loudly, caught in the mounting fury.

Tom presses the throttle harder, sensing the danger of the bike trying to grip the muddy surface, adrenalin pumping furiously through his body. Yet his mind is calm, detached in the swirling, chaotic consciousness. The boys are yelling something. He makes out their voices, faces and flashing arms, but is oblivious to any message, bound in his attempts to defy reality. The mud splashes his face; trees, bushes, faces, clouds, blackness, spinning before his eyes, the bike shuddering and jumping. Coldly pressing the throttle tighter, he smiles to himself, seeing the world trembling beneath his power. Lee is screeching, 'Stop the bloody thing, you stupid idiot, stop it, stop it.'

He tightens his grip which takes him back to another time; he's aware of the staring faces and the tightening arms; he remembers his mother's voice saying, 'Now don't be silly Tom, you can't fight us.' He's being carried now, something is shoved over his mouth, his arms are forced against each other. He hears voices, sees eyes, noses. 'He's a real nut this one.' Hearing that, he presses harder, defying the picture in his mind, blankly staring out into the meaningless sky.

Crash! Cutting agony. Blackness.

The boys stand immobile, re-enacting a slow motion of him heading straight into the fence, unable to grasp what has occurred before their eyes. Slowly, he regains consciousness, tastes the blood in his mouth, tries to move. The others pick him up, 'Yuh fuckin' fool, yuh could have killed yerself.'

'So what, it's my life.' He tenderly feels his bruised arm, turns and heads off, leaving them standing, staring at the twisted bike.

It's a Monday morning and Tom's in his English class. As usual the work handed out means little or nothing to him. He makes out a few scattered words. The English sheet is titled, 'Famous People, who were they, and what did they do to become famous?'

'Ff-am-o-uss', unable to blend the sounds, becomes 'fams-o-oss'.

'Pee-opal-lal,' recognizes the general sound of it, 'people' emerges. Something 'people'.

He looks around feeling obvious in his inability to read, having to mouth and hear the blending letters to make any sense of them. The teacher sits reading something up front, the kids are working on by themselves. He wants to scream out, 'I can't read it.'

'Something, fam-o-uss people' knowing how others speak it, 'ww', blocked by the 'w', knowing its sound, and the 'h' sound, yet they refuse to jell, being totally meaningless. 'ww-hh-oo'. He finds 'hhoo, hoe' then it occurs w-hoe, sounding firstly like woho, wo-who, then 'who' comes, from a memory sound again. His concentration span has ended, so he switches off, gets up and out of the chair and wanders around the room.

The teachers, reading and writing to a workable formula, are outside the worldview of the illiterate person. In this case, the English teacher, immersed in her newspaper, looks up to find Tom wandering blithely from one group to another. She interrupts, 'What do you think you're doing?' he shrugs, wandering on. She gets up, going to his desk. 'You've done nothing at all, this is simply not good enough.' He takes no notice outwardly, but inwardly he's tight and tense, afraid of another public humiliation. 'Now I'm talking to you Goodwood, don't just shrug your shoulders.' Shrug, knowing he has her measure in this type of communication. 'Don't shrug your shoulders at me.' She's red-faced and thinking, 'He must be stupid or something, he can't treat me this way.' Aloud, 'Now don't just stand there looking stupid, look at me when I talk to you.' Tom's reply is very clear 'Get stuffed.' He walks to the door. She screams out, 'What was that, what did you say? I'm not taking that, you're coming to the Vice-Principal with me.' Again, a calm clear, 'Get stuffed.' He walks out of the room, she moves to grapple with him. He turns to face her. She draws back, suddenly conscious of the cold, fixed stare, the taut body and clenched fists. 'He's a nut,' goes through her mind, yet to save face, she comes out with, 'Go on, get out, you're a delinquent, not fit for anything but a jail,' and slams the door in his face.

He speeds off, mentally cutting her to pieces with a monstrous hunting knife, feeling happier at every slash and scream, in the fantasy world of his mind.

Friday is another typically bad day for Tom.

There's a debate at breakfast about his clothes.

'Why wear that old grubby jacket? No, you're just not wearing it, I'll burn it.'

At school there's a collision in the corridor over the 'no way' sign. 'Who do you think you are? If you come here you obey the rules like the rest of us.'

At lunchtime there's a punch-up over a missing bike, 'I know you took it Goodwood, everybody says so.'

In the afternoon, there's a discussion with the police, 'What are you doing here fishing? You'll be up for truanting if you don't get back to school quick.'

Later there's a run-in with a shop attendant, 'Those bloody cigs you've got, I seen yuh take 'em.'

And at the beginning of the evening there's the usual nightly squabble with his sister, 'You always watch *your* cartoons. Mum says I can watch mine tonight.'

This is followed by the traditional squabble ritual with his mother about what's being watched on T.V., to be followed with, 'You're not going out again tonight' and 'I'm not going to keep putting up with you like this, you hear me.'

1976

January

Wednesday night

I pick up Tom and his friend from the flats, around 7 p.m. His mother wants to show me part of her struggle.

'He never does what I tell him to, he just goes his own way. I came in tonight and he was fighting with Katy again, punching her and calling her all sorts of things and he says them to me too . . .' She looks around to catch our attention and direct the focus in turn on Tom, who feigns disinterest. She goes on, 'My brothers would never have dared call my mum the things he calls me.'

I try to work out how to leave, taking with me Tom and the other boy who's a new face in the group and who is obviously being used by Tom as a strategic weapon. But Tom's mother demands a scene, wanting to show me something, though the timing is not quite right. Tom knows this.

'And you're too soft on him,' she awkwardly shouts in my direction, 'We're all too soft on him.'

Tom doesn't want me in the middle right now, so he plays her the line, 'Katy stole me cigs and me runners and wrecked one of 'em.'

His mother, now confident after gaining a momentary advantage, comes in harder, 'And who paid for them? I did. Who always pays for things?' Tom, intent on T.V., mutters 'Get fucked!' loud enough to disconcert her. Silence. His mother visibly reddens, whirls around on him. 'Don't you dare speak to me like that, you hear me? I had to put up with that from your father, but not from you.' He turns, looks her straight in the face, wavers slightly, then drops a look of blank indifference. She turns to me, 'I don't know why you bother with him, he's such a little pig sometimes, a little pig . . . I don't care anyway.'

We amble around after leaving the flats. Tom plays as if there's nothing wrong. The other boy sits silent and pensive. I grow hotter and hotter wishing to shake everyone in that household, past and present, and Tom knows my feelings. We play pool. I win. I play a few games with the other boy, letting him relax.

Later in the night Tom and I drive along the Altona foreshore; it's a chilly, foggy, sharp night. We have something to eat; the mood becomes lighter, easier, a bit playful, but still undermined by a desperate seriousness. He wrestles, bites, kicks. I grab his ankle; he fights back, laughing with hard steely eyes. I grip his ankle harder; he swings away and collapses face forward in the front passenger's seat.

I drive to the deserted beachfront and wait. Time draws on. He slowly starts to heave with emotion, twisting away into the corner. I know what to do now, play it by ear.

Later still I sit smoking one of his cigarettes. He wipes the tears from his face and whimpers, 'I wanna go home . . . will yuh take me home?'

'No'.

'I wanna go home to me mother.'

'Not this time, until we sort things out.'

'I'll walk.' He goes to open the door, I take his wrists away from it and hold them tight together. We enter the next stage; every muscle in his body tightens. His teeth grind audibly.

'Fuck off, fuck off, don't yuh touch me yuh cunt.' I

let his wrists go, yet block his exit. He tightens again, lowers the tone of his voice, 'Yuh're gonna get it bad boy . . . yuh'll be killed slowly.' And he turns on that feeling to stare me out, full faced. I stare back. Again, the sound of grinding teeth, again the clenching, tightening body, and then the explosion: a high-pitched wail, fluctuating in volume, then he rocks back and forth for about a minute or more.

I slap him hard across the face. He turns, his fists ready, his eyes full of fury. I say quietly, 'Come on hit me.' He screams back, 'I'll get me dad to get yuh.' I shrug my shoulders, he narrows his stare, his cheeks are all puffed up and his face is full of tears, 'I know where he is, in Footscray, and he'll get yuh real good.' A glint of sheer triumph.

I say, slowly and clearly, 'Where is he now, when you need him?'

This exposes the open wound; he falls shaking to the floor, crying loudly, twisting into a small, heaving heap. The deep crying goes on for a while, then stops. He buries himself deeper into the floor and sobs out, 'I'll kill the bastard, I'll kill 'im, I'll kill 'im, I'll slit 'is throat, I'll kill 'im for what he did to me mum [now rocking, moaning], bashin' 'er all the time. I'll get 'im yuh'll see. I'll get him in a pub. I'll be real friendly then I'll knife 'im in the back and slit his throat, [slower now] the blood will be all over me and I'll rub it all over me hands and eyes and . . .'

I interrupt, 'You bloody liar, you're nothing but a bloody liar.'

He turns, white-faced with rage, 'Don't yuh believe me? Yuh'll see yuh cunt.'

Slowly, I say 'You're not really worried about your mum, it's what he did to you, Tom, when he walked out and left.'

'I'll kill 'im, I'll kill the . . .' He collapses, pleading, 'Take me home to me mum, please, I wanna go home.'

I sit and wait. Twenty minutes pass, he whimpers a bit and then there's silence.

He turns, looks me hard and straight in the face, 'John, will yuh help me with me work this term at school? The others try to make me mad and throw a fit. I trust you.'

I look him straight in the face, 'Yes.'

Friday night

I am at the Coffee Shop. There are about one hundred and fifty kids there, varying in age from twelve to the mid-twenties. The Coffee Shop is an attraction for latch-key kids, the social misfits, the unemployed and the unemployable. A group arrives to break up the place, but when they discover they are acceptable here, they decide to leave it intact and make it their home. Many others have found their way there; girls and boys from violent backgrounds seeking a caring locality, not to mention the many lost, drunk and hurt kids.

Several local adults work here voluntarily on Friday nights. Rosemary runs it and the energy and animation of the place comes from her. She has an uneasy relationship with the other adults. Kids, old and young, flock around her, tell her stories of their conquests, their escapes, their run-ins, invite her to the local poolroom to teach her pool. They come back on Saturday mornings to help her fix the place up and to be with her.

Rosemary is in her early thirties, a large woman who has straight, almost accusing eyes. She is determined to help the discarded children and youth around her. She comes from a traditional, strong, caring, working-class family. She helped to support her sisters and brother through school when she went out to work at the age of thirteen. Her world revolves around the children that no one else wants or can be bothered with. To Rosemary, they are not the emotional cripples society has made them out to be. They are simply children who need love and care.

I am getting to know Rosemary as a fellow traveller and intimate friend. We share the same frustrations, the same let-downs and sense of isolation. She has worked one-to-one with knotted, desperate children. Often after a hard Friday night, Rosemary and I take a group of girls and boys down to the local pizza parlour, have something to eat, talk through problems and play some pool. This is where I learn so much about the lives of these children and what they carry inside them when they enter school, jobs and inevitably court.

Friday night, a week later

As usual, I am at the Coffee Shop. Tom comes in drunk, or at least, with the pretence of being drunk. Looking back, I think I was aware of the forces swelling up to the explosion that followed. I can see him caught up in the claustrophobic atmosphere. You can't live on the edge of a sword for ever. And the pressure on him is becoming unbearable.

Through the alcoholic haze he hears someone say, 'Sammy and Lee are gonna fight the Footscray gunnies. They're gonna shoot 'em too.'

It's exaggerated gossip, but Tom's mind is jaded. He remembers his breakdown in the gym in front of his mates, his tears of frustration and his collapse. If he doesn't go along with them now, he'll be letting them down. He is being shoved and hassled by the claustrophobic atmosphere. The situation demands a gesture from him. He races off to help them, caught up in tears of rage. I hear a boy call out, 'Yuh always start cryin'.' For Tom, that is the flashpoint.

I follow Tom down to the moonlit beach, through the dark, stony carparks. He is running madly, drunkenly, in an attempt to restore some safety to his inner self.

There follow two hours of verbal hell . . .

'Let me go, let me go, yuh're too good to be shot, I'm bad, let me go . . .'

His tone changes, growing hateful and cunning. I block him and he tightens inside himself and screeches at me. 'I'll kill yuh, I'll fuckin' well kill yuh . . .' His tone changes. It's quieter and almost menacing. 'I'll rip yer eyeballs out and twist the blade into yer brain.' Everything comes out, the self-hate, the projected hatred, the venom from old wounds. It spurts out. He's squirming, writhing, screaming. He's really frustrated with me. He wants to get at me somehow.

Later in the car near the flats he acts out the murder of my family, hurt friends and anyone else close to me, before racing off and locking himself in the toilet at the flat. Eventually, I carry him to bed, limp and wrung out.

Has the damage been uncovered this time?

Tuesday

Today we are at a distance from each other. Deep hurts, hidden feelings have come out. He draws back, looks hard at me, I hope time is on my side.

Thursday

This can't keep going, I'll do something to break the bind, anything . . .

We are caught, snared in our fixed roles, rigid inside as if in suits of armour. I am hoping for some relief. I wonder if he can handle our genuine, honest exchanges now. Will they rebound in my face?

When is the moment ripe for movement and change?

February

Friday

I arrive home to find a letter for me from the Education Department. They are making me 'an offer I can't refuse'. I must teach for one year at Werribee Tech. and then they will let me work full-time the following year with the kids at Williamstown. It is a clear and unequivocal statement from one of the top administrators in technical education.

Tuesday

My transfer was made effective immediately, so I am now working at Werribee as the third form humanities teacher. But have I been conned? Was the offer genuine? I've just discovered that the man who effected the conditions of my transfer has gone overseas on study leave. New conditions and determinants may arise. How can I retain my links with the Williamstown kids, especially Tom?

Friday

I haven't seen Tom for a few weeks. Tonight he came to find me at the Coffee Shop, a face at the door. He wants contact and safety again. We play together and our growing bond reasserts itself.

Wednesday night

I decide to go to see the local humanities inspector at the Department of Technical Education to clarify the promises made about where I would be teaching next year. I had sent in numerous letters to which I had received no replies.

Who will take the responsibility for a past agreement now? After even telephone calls failed to produce a response, an American friend who teaches with me at Werribee suggests I go in and confront them face to face. So I go; we talk and share our experiences in schools and life. I ask him to clear up the terms of the agreement.

Nothing concrete comes out of it.

Am I acting on a past faith with these people? I try to stretch supportive words and use them as a basis for believing actions will follow. It is easy to get wrapped up in their smiles and words.

Sunday

Tom and I and some of the other kids are working on an old car.

The night is dark; it is fresh, cool and crisp; a new autumn frost is forming; the lights sparkle from the sky. The purples and yellows against the skyline, the outlines of dusty brick houses, the noises of cars and people, and a slight chilly breeze, all combine to form a whole impression of the delicacy of life's movements.

I am aware that I have created this situation. I watch it, observe it, become part of it, move away from it, experience the range of feelings, the softness, the give and take, and the gentle pushing and shoving.

The sullen aftermath is yet to come.

March

Monday

Tom moves to the local high school annexe. Lisa

Golding knew about the work being done there with a group of twenty or so rejected kids from surrounding schools. The technical school is no place for a child beginning to find his feet in the world.

But what is my role now in Tom's world? Being no longer his special teacher, though I was never only that, I have become part of his most intimate adult–child struggle.

Tuesday night

I am standing outside the Coffee Shop in front of my car. Suddenly this dark, large object producing a loud, spluttering sound appearing to be heading my way careers across the nearest intersection. I stare, stunned momentarily, and see, to my chilled horror, Tom perched ridiculously at the wheel of a broken-down, moth-eaten 1956 Holden. 'Over the fence and fast' flashes through my mind. The Holden is swerving, over and under steering, travelling fast. I go over the fence; it stops short, just twenty centimetres clear. Out gets Tom followed by half a dozen young, beaming, vocal kids.

He cannot give up these things he acquires. The old deserted car, the stolen mini-bike; he just can't give them up. 'I've got 'em now ... they're mine.' For Tom it is almost unbearable to part with the pleasure that ownership gives him.

Wednesday

Tom has spells of sudden playfulness. He wants to play, fight, wrestle. The emerging pattern in our play is something like: push, receive, push back, receive, and retreat; then push, receive, push back, receive, this time in a sulky way and without the final retreat.

There is a clearcut learning experience expressed

within this pattern. He pushes, then holds back on himself and learns to grasp a little more of his own identity each time. He takes a larger risk every time.

But what is the crucial scene towards which all our play and work is heading? I still think it is to bring the boy face to face with his long-gone father. I am convinced that what I call his 'learning paralysis' is rooted here.

Certainly any attempts to unlock the paralysis can only come from the close intimacy already established between us, yet a fixed barrier still seems to be there. It will take a huge risk or jab to move it.

Thursday night

We talk and play. He says something ugly about a friend and I poke him slightly harder. He tenses and walks away in a huff. This is only one tiny aspect of all the things we are working through.

I wonder how much is unchangeable in a child. Is the genetic influence stronger than the environmental one? And what about the factors endemic to any one family? How much can change?

Friday

Rosemary, Lee and I arrange to go out for tea. Lee wants to see us privately.

At Rosemary's, Lee comes in followed by Tom. Tom goes straight through the house, hardly says anything to Rosemary and demands to be part of what we are going to do. I say, 'No, we'll see you after our meal with Lee.' He heads off. Rosemary, taking her car around the back, sees him in tears, heaving deeply with emotion, crying like a rejected baby.

I don't know, sometimes I wonder about myself and what I do. I think I know a little of the cold, anxiety building up in him and his explosive pressure cycle.

My rejection has cut and hurt him. He doesn't want me to see him hurt and hear him cry. His sense of being an outsider brings him to near desperation. What am I doing to his self-image?

As I have said to Rosemary, what I did was right in a family setting but perhaps it's wrong in the present disjointed situation. Right, but wrong.

Wednesday

Things have really started to move again. We are having play therapy sessions. At times Tom becomes a playful, cuddling baby, at other times a seven-year-old boy playing with his father, and then at others, a sensually aware fourteen-year-old stretching out to the limits of his world. He can take more stress, wants to play and act out the distrust and his self-contempt.

His mother finds the reversions and acting out hard to take. She wants him to communicate sensibly, like a proper fourteen-year-old boy should be able to. I talk with her about his stages of behaviour and how she might cope with them.

Wednesday night, a week later

Tonight Tom doesn't extend his play therapy sessions at home, thereby partially acknowledging his mother's needs. He plays like a fourteen-year-old, not as an exuberant seven-year-old. He wants to show me something of his family and produces the family football album. He looks, walks, speaks less rigidly; he now has a growing self-assurance.

Earlier we drove around and chatted about things; a good full dialogue. He took me on a personal journey into his past: around the world of his father's family, along the escape routes from the Institution to his home, and into the things he felt. 'I don't trust many people;

you, Lee and sometimes Mum.' This working through is the only way to restore the praxis of the inner and outer self in the world, that is, the wholeness I believe is necessary for survival.

Our play together, the physical contact growing between us in the safety of our trust frees him to express himself and to develop and communicate in new ways. The walls are pushed back and a small exploration is made: growth.

Friday

Tom's separation from his mother, the disruption when he was put in an Institution was the crucial break in his history. 'She let 'em take me' is the basis of his trauma in terms of the disjointed father–son and husband–wife settings.

Was the real damage done here? Being deserted by his mother after the earlier loss of his father has left a semi-permanent scar which affects his capacity to trust, learn and love.

Sunday night

We visit his father's parents. They haven't seen him for a long time. It's a good amiable meeting. His grandmother is immediately friendly, brewing cups of tea, talking with one of her neighbours and Tom's aunt at the kitchen table. His grandfather is working-class and more reserved, and his face is lined from years of physical toil. He slowly opens up and finally I get him to talk about his work around Swan Hill in the depression days and the techniques of illegal cod netting in the Murray River.

Tom starts the evening anxiously, carrying unpleasant memories. He clearly shows the need for some personal acceptance. After a few nervous moments he settles in. His father is never mentioned. I have heard he lives around Footscray, holding down an occasional job in between bouts of booze and violence. Tom's aunt is friendly, yet I sense she is tough and hard bitten.

We stay for a couple of hours. As I talk with his grandparents Tom wanders around, watching the T.V. in the lounge room, feeling free from the tensions he used to feel here. He enjoys the experience of being there in his own right. By coming back in this way, he has closed off the possibility of being hurt by the rejection he once felt here and carried inside himself for years. He looks freer and more relaxed afterwards than at any time I can remember. I see tonight's small transformation as a slow, hesitant, forward movement.

A re-working of some earlier traumas now seems possible. Tom's reaction to interruptions in his relationship with his mother and others close to him is the framework I must use to help him work through his blocks, his paralysis.

I need to study the period he was in the Institution in relation to the time his father left and the emotional state of his mother at the time, for instance, did she need Tom to be in the Home for 'a breathing space'? I must also consider his school situation at the time.

I must go deeper into Tom's mother's statement that he was extremely distressed the first few times she went to visit him in the Home. In fact his departure had been highly traumatic. Tom thought his mother 'let him go'. He was intuitively correct. I suspect Tom's mother, then in her late twenties, was in a desperate, powerless situation. The young boy sensed this at the time and lost trust in her. She says he was different after being institutionalized. He tried to run away three times. What an incredible bind!

Was he in this bind when I first saw him last year?

Did this cause the alternating over-demanding, hostile, withdrawn behaviour I saw then? The linchpin of his actions is his refusal to trust people — this fits in with his mother's occasional, though devastating, comments that she can't control him, that he might possibly have to go back to the Home again. He knew he had been rejected once and was liable to be rejected again. Hence, his realistic fear of forming any close relationships.

April

Wednesday

Tom's mother is upset. His father has contacted a relative and the news has travelled back down the family grapevine that he has been enquiring about his son.

I can see all the old traumas, rejections, needs and defeats on her face. We talk, things come out, snippets of devastating experiences. She re-lives moments of her past.

I hear about the night her husband came home drunk. He ran over the lawnmower in the driveway at about 3 a.m., came in cursing Tom in his stupor for leaving it there, got Tom out of bed and threw him out into the backyard.

She told me about the fears she had about him coming back, buying the kids off with gifts she could not afford: 'I've done all the work . . .'

The truth was that he beat her night after night; and now she says, 'I stayed with him for six years, I can't think how . . . I'll kill him if he comes back for the kids . . . when we had a fight, at any time in the night, he'd get the kids, especially Tom, up to see it . . . he'd bash him sometimes . . . he cut his face open one time out of sheer spite.'

What did it do to Tom to watch these things?

Friday

At Easter we go camping at Torquay. Food and beer cans are scattered among the tents. Rosemary, Lee, Tom and Patrick are getting ready to leave. I am clearing up. Lee, Tom and Patrick sit in the car. We argue about a bike that had been left nearby. The boys had just used it until the owner came to collect it. I am left negotiating with the owner while they sit in the car. When the owner finally leaves, Tom gets out and jumps on the bonnet. I tell him to get off it. He just sits there. I get a bucket of water, having intended to clean a few things, but throw the water on him; he slithers to the ground, shaken. He gets back in the car and won't leave it, he just sits there.

Slowly a good natured humour emerges; it is the first time he has faced his own actions in this way.

Thursday

When I first met Tom, he lived mainly in fantasy. He still lives in this haze at times. For example, after our last confrontation, he wanted to feel good about our relationship. He told Rosemary a tale of great imagination and detail. He knew I was going down to Ocean Grove to help my brother-in-law with some plumbing. In his story, he was the hero, digging up a backyard, working from five in the morning until ten at night setting up an entire sewerage system, working arm in arm with me. 'It makes him feel good to say these things,' Lee said.

I asked Tom about it later. 'I don't have to talk if I don't wanna.'

After this he produced a deep, warming smile, something he increasingly falls back on. He is beginning to learn to use adult responses in a protective and useful way.

Tom has begun to write a story for me.

Friday

Tonight he acts out the way he sees his own behaviour. Step by step, line by line, movement for movement. 'This is what I'll do next and yuh'll say . . .' and half-smiling rolls himself up in a ball in the corner and plays 'mum'. I sit staggered, thinking about it: his behaviour is a learned response, an ingrained reflex, a strategy for survival, a means of support. What if he is gradually placed in a secure relationship where he doesn't need these old defences any more? The clothes no longer fit.

Sunday

I have found out, accidentally, that Tom knows some boys' mothers who believe in the occult. They told Tom that dogs bark furiously at 'possessed' people. He had a great fear of dogs after this. They told him about the 'painted bird', the outsider of the flock that risks being pecked to death, and he identifies with it.

I feel very angry that these people have told him these things: that he has a mask of death, that he will kill someone. It reinforces the boy's deepest death wishes towards his father. Why should he have this extra burden placed upon him? What damage will it do to his psyche, carrying this awful designation, as if it is a script to be acted out? I see it as part of the local community's vicious stigmatization.

I have to release him from this burden with safety and love. The knowledge of what has been done can be used to free him from it.

Monday night, 5.30

We have arranged to meet. He doesn't roll up. I leave a note. I WAIT FOR NOBODY. JOHN.

Later I am out with Lee and we find him in the local pizza parlour. He pretends to be guilty but laughs. I explode, 'Get out! I don't want to see you for a while.' He breaks down and yells out, 'Fuck off.' I go out for some cool air.

I want him to face up to the implications of his broken agreement. It has made me angry. He must learn to make an adult commitment and stick to it. Right back at the start of our relationship Tom said, 'They all leave me and I see I'm bad.' In the past I've allowed Tom to get away with this sort of statement but tonight I feel I must stay and take the risk.

It turns into a wild night. Lee and I find Tom near the flats where he lives. He runs away from us. We follow him and he hides in the trees behind the flats. We finally catch up with him and he wants to fight both of us. He struggles, bites and throws himself around. I have had enough of it all. He wants Lee to give him back his knife. Lee is frightened to give it to him knowing that he has slashed people before in similar moments of stress. I say, 'Give it to him, Lee!' Tom looks at it, opens it, runs his finger down the blade. I sit on the grass with Lee and ignore him. Minutes pass. Tom walks around us holding his knife. Suddenly he flicks it shut and sits down with us. His face is terribly haggard and he wears his guilt. I take the conversation away from what has happened. We talk about other things.

Wednesday

The police are getting the kids to tell on each other. Tom is to be charged with receiving stolen goods — two fishing rods. Unknown to me, he has been truanting again. He is stopped by the police at a local railway station, taken to the police station and forced to make a statement. He is left with the threat that he will be put in Baltara next time they find him skipping school. They label him a compulsive liar and a weak character.

There's a big scene at home. Tom sits hunched and hostile in the corner of the room. His mother swings from expressions of despair to shrill anger. I feel that Tom is still holding back the truth and I am privately angry about this break in our trust. I want the truth no matter what.

Although Tom has only known me for just over a year, he holds a deep affection for me and he knows I care for him, so why is he avoiding telling me the truth?

On top of all this, earlier in the afternoon I found him with Tony on a 'hot' bike. He and Tony wouldn't even discuss it with me. I told them the cops were on the prowl; yet, caught in their self-destructive web they still went off on the bike. I am incredibly angry.

Thursday

Tom is at the Coffee Shop in a pensive mood. He is now outside the older group which is closing its ranks in the wake of the mounting police blitz; he is a loner, untrusted and unwanted. He heads off with the same group of younger boys he knows dobbed him in to the police over truanting. Since Lee Waxford, his peer group leader and personal tutor, cut him dead in front of the others, he needs these younger boys, no matter what the consequences.

I speak to him later about a few trivial things; reassured that I still care, he goes home for the night.

May

Sunday

I see Tom at the pool and pinball room. He looks pleased to see me but his expression changes when he sees some other boys come in to see me. He shoots off with them saying, 'Can I see yuh tomorrow night?' I feel like a lifeline in a wild sea.

Monday

I am phoned at Werribee and told that Tom is not at school. Later I discover he's not at home either. I go to the police station with his mother to get a copy of the statement they took from Tom when they charged him with receiving stolen goods.

He comes home later, friendly, yet shallow. We play a bit, I say, 'I care for you very much Tom, and you're wrecking our relationship.' I give him three remedial English books and he talks openly about missing the last couple of days at school. As I leave, another boy, distressed and shaken, comes to see me. Tom sees the other child's need and this time isn't possessive about me.

Tuesday

I call in at the flat to find Tom's mother going out. The children are watching T.V.

I reflect on the constant problems for a person working with someone designated a 'problem child'; every time you're with them you encounter new variables. You have to learn to cope with them as they arise. Sometimes it's exhausting.

I sit with the children. Katy is throwing verbal darts. Tom is caught in my presence and his role. The feeling remains: nothing can ever be taken for granted here. It's hard work all the way.

Later we play, talk about school and the books Tom is reading, and he acts out the mimic routine again. 'Excuse me, I'll be right in about three hours so you'll just have to put up with me.' [Laughter]

He takes over the adult's role, 'Now pull yourself out of it, don't be silly . . . do yuh want me to have to treat you like a child.' I roll around more furiously, thrashing like a mad dog, yelling, 'Let me go, let me go.' He puts on the mask of threatening authority, interspersed with giggles and laughter. His face is open and responsive.

Wednesday

He reads for nearly two hours, enjoys the exercises that I give him to match symbols with pictures, draws cartoons and plays a few word games.

At moments he lifts one mask revealing another older but at once younger and more self-accepting child. He is learning to give.

I leave to go to another engagement.

Thursday

Tom has been picked up by the police. After school I find out the details. About lunchtime he was out on a school friend's mini-bike and saw the police at a distance. When he realized it was Detective Briggs, the cop who got him for 'receiving' offences last week, he panicked, reminded of their threat to put him straight back into Baltara next time they saw him out of school. Tom fled. The police charged after him. Tom went down a one-way street the wrong way, was forced to crash the bike, and was arrested and booked on four counts: riding an unregistered bike, driving without a licence, failing to wear a safety-helmet and driving in a dangerous fashion.

I had arranged to visit Lisa Golding with Tom tonight, but he won't come, just hangs his head, defeated and beaten down. He oscillates between capitulation (it is safer to give up and get locked up) and the real fear of being deserted and cut off. He is moving very slowly, like a bruised fighter.

I simply say, 'All right, it's up to you. I'm going, see you later.'

I discuss with Lisa the double charges, the luck of which magistrate hears the case, the need to reassure Tom that we care and won't desert him, and that the rest is up to him.

I see Tom later on and tell him I have spoken to Lisa, that she knows the scene and she would really like to see him when he feels like it.

We sit and talk about many things. A more self-assured boy emerges. His eyes are clear, he is more willing to give and take, and his presence is very different from the earlier regressed and anxious boy.

Sunday

I meet Lisa. She has been in contact with a former social worker of Tom's. Evidently his work was good until third grade when his father left and he had been a happy, bouncy child. After his father left, Tom retreated like a shell-shocked soldier and became, according to this person, 'a grossly victimized boy, in and out of the classroom'.

Sunday night, a week later

We're out for an easy, relaxed night, playing pool, pinball, riding high, carefree in the world. But then there's a sudden switch off. I am deeply bewildered. I feel angry, expecting more after all the confrontations we've worked through. I am still caught as though stunned in a spotlight by his sudden reversals of form. I feel as though his behaviour tonight is a précis of his whole life-cycle. Thinking about it, it seems to me the tension at home, the torn parent–child relationship was interrupted by my entry into Tom's world; our immediate affinity and bond eased the hostility between mother and son.

When I take him to another environment where he can be happy and playful he shows moments of pure animation, yet they are constantly interspersed with erratic flashes of meanness and agitated violence. Tom would withdraw, then explode with rage, and fight anyone within range. Exhausted by the release of tension he would break down, then gradually subside into stillness and calm. Contact would be restored. We would be moving forward again.

It's a struggle to release the hidden springs of our existence.

Thursday

The thing is really moving. Among the moments of indecision and dislocation there are times of uninhibited animation and restful calm. The long involved talks about work, fun, sex, what people think, and why I act as I do, are beginning to make sense.

In the last six months Tom has started to read and write again. There have been massive upheavals, almost radical changes in his self-perception.

Friday

He is really working at school for the first time. He reads a page or more every night for me. I demand truthfulness and constancy and attempt to work through the things that seem to create blocks in his relationships with the world.

We had planned to have a reading session tonight but an incident during the day disturbed him and threw him off his track. He becomes erratic and hostile with his mother and me. He forces his mother to a showdown, a window is broken. His mother leaves in tears and rage. I stay.

His mother seemed lost and defeated, yet I feel real movement underneath. Tom breaks down very quickly with me, crying like a hurt baby, something he does not do now in front of others. His pattern of confrontation–breakdown–release can be all over in thirty minutes now, unlike the hours-long sessions of the past.

Sunday

Today is another day of broken arrangements. Tom refuses to explain anything. I get angry. Tom explodes with rage, breaks down and cries and then we begin to talk again.

My words seem to affect him deeply for when I am angry with him he screws up his face, finds it hard to look straight at me and fidgets with anything handy.

June

Wednesday night

Tom wants and needs someone to help him to order his life, to take charge of certain parts of his personality, to say 'no' specifically at times and mean it, to direct him at times, to let go at other moments . . .

Our relationship at this juncture is based on Tom's need for my authority. He needs me to set limits for him . . . Where does this take us in the future?

I am now confronted by the prospect of Tom being locked up again, so I am mustering whatever evidence I can to prevent this happening. I decide to ask Rosemary Heathcote, youth coordinator at the Coffee Shop to write a supporting statement for the court.

Rosemary has worked for twenty years with kids like Tom and she has the advantage of having lived and worked in Williamstown all her life. As well, I consider her to be constructively blunt, tough and honest. She is, quite simply, the best person to ask. This is her statement.

The effects of an emotional crisis on a child can be many and varied. In the case of Tom Goodwood, an apparently bright youngster, a learning paralysis occurred at the time of his parents' parting. School reports lead us to believe that at the age of seven Tom was a good twelve months further advanced than his school grading suggested, especially with reading. At this very moment we have a fourteen-and-a-half year old boy who is just resuming the learning process at a seven or eight-year-old level.

The last eighteen months of Tom's life have been far from easy. In fact you could say that they have been filled with traumatic experiences which, on many occasions, have left him, after working through problems with the help of John Embling, absolutely drained of energy. A boy that has had a learning paralysis for seven or more years is the victim of many constant pressures, one of the heaviest being the peer group scene. It is difficult to imagine oneself not being able to read a street sign, the instructions on a bottle of medicine, the warning on a packet of poison or the headlines of the daily news; these are just a few of the problems Tom faces daily. It goes without saying that the ridicule and hurt that can be inflicted by a group of teenagers (with this sort of knowledge about a fellow student) can be intolerable.

The pressure from the home and school environment can also be very painful. It is very humiliating constantly to have the achievements of younger members of your family and fellow students thrown in your face. To add to the many other pressures placed on the lad, at the age of ten-and-a-half years Tom was placed in the maximum security section of Baltara Boys' Home under a protection order. Over a six to eight month period he headed off for home on three or four occasions, which is surely a normal instinct, only to be returned by his mother and placed in an even more secure location. It is interesting to note that truancy was the major thing that the boy had against him, and it makes one wonder just how an offence of this nature (if indeed it is one in an emotionally disturbed child) warrants time in a cell with only a mattress for company. Solitary confinement is responsible for the breaking of many hardened criminals. God only knows how it screws up the mind of a ten-year-old. Extreme fear of officialdom of any sort and lack of faith and trust in anyone are just two of the many side-effects of Tom's institutionalization.

I couldn't even make a rough guess of the amount of time, energy and patience expended by Tom and John going through crisis after crisis in the last eighteen months in order to start the learning and emotional growth cycle moving again. In fact it has only been in the last three or four weeks that Tom has started to move tentatively out of his almost autistic world, where he retreats into a world of silence and often curls up in a corner, and into a new world in which he feels safe to explore his feelings and try out new relationships. He is moving slowly, but surely forward, through the lost years of emotional growth and learning. Tom has great difficulty in handling anything other than a one-to-one relationship and not many of these are successful because of his lack of faith and trust in human nature. This fact alone is one of the many reasons that his present support group (psychological guidance officer, teacher, personal counsellor) need to be constantly aware that one interruption to the new stages he is entering could cause a disastrous set back.

In closing I pass the comment that without the untiring patience and remarkable persistence of John Embling, Tom would still be in his autistic shell. The bond between the two has grown steadily stronger through each crisis. John's role varies from father-figure to playmate, back to teacher and then perhaps on to counsellor and confessor. Regardless of the role he is playing at any one time, he is a figure who has proved to Tom that he will not forsake him in time of crisis. To a lesser degree the same things apply to the integrated studies teacher, Lloyd Wicknall, and his psychological guidance officer, Lisa Golding. Tom does not need more psychologists, teachers, magistrates or probation officers, but he surely needs the opportunity to work on through his present growing and strengthening relationships.

Thursday

Tom breaks another arrangement and we have another row. 'I don't give no promises no more anyway. I change me mind if I wanna. It's my business. What's it to you anyway?'

Even Tom's mother wonders if I am placing too much pressure on him. 'He's real difficult at times, just like his father was. It's not worth the effort; he just does what he likes. I hope it's worth all your effort.'

Friday

Tom's mother is defensive, fearing yet another repeat performance of Tom freaking out because of the pressures mounting on him as his court appearance approaches. She is afraid he'll run away. Tom is sitting against the lounge room heater; quiet, pensive and frightened. He goes out. I talk with his mother.

Later that night Tom and I meet at the Coffee Shop. Other kids flock around. He comes closer, speaks, shoves me playfully. We talk slowly, opening up, easing out, and something rattles away in my brain about Tom and his mother being denied a loving relationship with each other by a harsh, uncaring world.

Saturday

I ask Tom if he wants to come to Geelong. He hedges around the question and says, 'I'm not comin''. I merely shrug my shoulders. He hesitates, then says, 'Let's go, I wanna see a movie.'

We watch a depressing, violent film about women in prison. He starts to talk about Baltara, about being locked up at night. I wonder if that has produced a basic, perhaps lasting insecurity. He still can't sleep alone in a strange room. I must move carefully here, this is a testing point. Yet I feel he is heading towards some real freedom. He is terribly vulnerable and fragile and needs a strong caring relationship.

Sunday

I am becoming increasingly aware that Tom has an urgent need for some basic physicality in his life. A lot of middle-class welfare workers and teachers shy away from this in their work with children from working-class backgrounds, somehow caught between their moralism about the brutality of many working-class teachers and policemen and their own middle-class fear of physical contact.

I think it's about time Tom learnt how to manage some of the practical problems of living. For instance, he's got absolutely no idea how other people handle money. His idea of budgeting goes something like this: spend the money you've got on cigarettes, grog, pinball, pool and then steal what more you need from under the milk bottles. We sit down together and calculate how much money he really needs each week.

Tuesday

Tom doesn't come as arranged but arrives about 10 p.m. He produces a story about hurting his thumb and asks me to wrap it up for him. But the story grows thin as he takes in the unsympathetic faces. He's confronted by a group of disbelieving people, his mother, his sister and me, and it soon becomes obvious to him that we are not prepared to suspend our disbelief. I grow restless and leave. Perhaps I am at fault for not following through the usual sequence of things.

Wednesday

After spending a weird night with Sammy and Tony I go to the Goodwoods'. Tom is at home, not saying much, obviously annoyed at my presence which makes him feel guilty and regretful. We go for a drive. He seems determined to have a scene with me because he wants the limelight. At least it's his own. There's a mild confrontation followed by his ritual breakdown. He heaves with emotion, 'I can't help it John, all these funny sorts of things make me act strange. The kids ask me why I've changed. Will I do a job with 'em?' It's the usual stuff: the let-down, the guilt, the drama and the tears of relief. Although the pattern is clearly starting to alter and the time sequences are different, the fundamentals still seem to be immovable.

In retrospect I can see a pattern in all our earlier work. It begins with Tom shrugging his shoulders and muttering abusive asides. 'Go away will yuh, I don't want yuh. I'll do meself in. I don't care. I don't trust anyone. I don't need anyone. Yuh shit me. I don't have to talk. I'm sayin' nothin'. I'm sayin' nothin'.' I just sit, shrug my shoulders and say, 'It's up to you Tom.' He fidgets, looks anywhere but at me, then collapses — heaving, sobbing, curling up in a ball, crying quietly. Then he looks straight into my face, usually asking, 'John, can we go for a drive?' or 'Can we do some readin'?' or 'Why do . . ?' Yet in some ways he is younger, like a trusting seven-year-old boy, open-faced and in need of constant reassurance. I still can't break the pattern and I must help him do this if he is to emerge as a healthy human being.

Thursday

Tom and Rusty are playing pinball. Rusty, an eleven-year-old understudy of a local gang leader, wants to keep playing, trying to beat the system, even though it's rigged to create the illusion that you can beat it. He pressurizes Tom to adhere to the stereotyped behaviour expected of him by his peer group and Tom acquiesces.

Tom is aware of all this because afterwards, when I drive him home, he says quietly to me, 'Was I hurtful to yuh?'

Friday

Tom comes to Geelong by himself. When he arrives at my place he says he doesn't want to play pinball. Only last week he told me, 'It must be in me blood. Me dad used to play it all the time.' We talk about his growing realization that his friends use him. He asks me, 'Why do the others get off for the same things? They never went in a Home last time. I never thought they'd all dob on me like they did.'

He's playful, and he's becoming more philosophical, more understanding about other people's shortcomings.

Sunday

Tom comes to see my sister and her newly arrived baby at the Geelong Hospital. He finds the family setting invigorating; he even seems relaxed and happy within the conventions and mannerisms of another family setting.

Later, on the way back to Williamstown, we clash. We stop for some fast food at Werribee but when Tom sees it isn't 'take away' he goes back to the car and leaves me with the lot.

'Why?', I ask. After a few tense moments he replies, 'I don't like people watchin' me eat.' We talk about honesty and working together to overcome these problems rather than just switching on and off like a light.

We call in at Rosemary's. She tells me later that when we arrived Tom said to her, 'thank you for bein' so kind and writin' me a reference for court.'

Over the weekend there were many revealing incidents, small snippets of past experiences or what Tom calls 'flashbacks I have in me mind'.

'Yuh know that wallet we gave yuh for Christmas? We stole it.' He showed me how he used to write 'so as to fool the shits at school who thought I was real dumb'.

He is striving for genuine honesty in his relationship with me. Most of the energy and direction is coming from him now. Can we keep this going without his peer group rejecting him destructively or without any critical blow-ups at school? And what about the forthcoming court appearance? I believe our relationship at the moment is as strong and resilient as it has ever been.

Monday

Tom breaks his collarbone at school. I learn about it when I turn up at his place but I have to leave with Rosemary to collect Lisa's court statement. Tom's case has been listed to be heard on Friday. We tell Tom's mother about Friday and she becomes nauseated and dizzy. We take her to the Footscray Hospital casualty department.

It is a night of insights. Tom, who cries like a hurt baby during our moments of tearing emotion, presents a stoic front, hardly showing any feelings of pain from his very sore shoulder. Evidently he had refused an injection earlier in the day and left hospital saying, 'I'm gonna meet John.'

Now it's his mother's turn: she feels dizzy and numb and needs care and reassurance. Her children are coping well. Tom certainly has strength in his character, regardless of what the police and staff at school say. As usual they see only the superficial things. And their failure to perceive anything deeper applies to many professionals as well — teachers, psychologists, social workers. Their only 'insight' comes from the results of I.Q. tests, behaviour assessments and consensus opinions. The clinical approach too often ignores that only a caring relationship can help children like Tom Goodwood. I want to understand the child's feelings and reactions and view of things.

This is what I see as the most promising approach to work with hurt and knotted children: start with the child's basic physicality concentrating on the initial feelings as they are expressed, then work through the child's blocks and traumas while constantly re-evaluating what is going on. I believe it is important to form a relationship with the child that is honest and physically secure and then to work uncompromisingly through the conflicts.

Once a trauma has been located it must be worked on and diffused.

Tuesday, Wednesday, Thursday nights

Three days of fluctuations, frustrations, excuses to give up, new elements, pressures, fears. I don't follow any predetermined script, I just play it as it comes.

At the moment Tom crouches near me, fragile, scared of the impending court appearance. He is afraid and cautious. His mother says many times, 'I fear they'll put him in the Home again.' His eyes are fearful, they speak of desertion. Why should he trust anyone? Trust is an empty, hollow word. Perhaps it's better to be certain that you're on your own. At least that's absolute. Memories of last time, the cold terror of being locked up alone, keep swirling around in his head.

In the Goodwood household the children strive desperately, often savagely, for ascendency over their mother. Even play and fun are full of nerve-racking tension and can turn, with the slightest change of mood, into a serious, deadly contest. Tom struggles within these confines to deal with his inner mounting pressures.

One of the major difficulties for a worker in this field is that every family has a different working dynamic demanding flexible and malleable approaches and responses from the worker.

Friday

I collect Tom and his mother from the flats and we meet Rosemary and a barrister I'd engaged, outside the Footscray Children's Court. At the beginning of the proceedings Tom and his mother are very nervous. I am aware this is a very important time for Tom. He needs to discover that he has a strong and dependable support group. During the hearing the police play a heavy, uncompromising authoritarian role, constantly asserting, 'The boy is no good.' We needed the barrister so we could play the legal game. It was as if we needed an interpreter; not to have used one would have guaranteed instant condemnation of Tom's actions and his automatic return to the Home. For a kid like Tom, undefended means guilty.

Tom is placed on a twelve months' good behaviour bond.

Saturday

Tom comes to Geelong for the weekend. On the way down we have a bad scene, a delayed response, I think, to the weeks of mounting tension that preceded the court appearance. 'I don't know what to think,' Tom says. His shoulder hurts and he shakes uncontrollably. 'I'll put meself in the Home. I'll get me mother to put me there. I'll nag her until she does. I don't need yer help anyway. I don't owe nobody nothin'. I'm cold.'

Too much force, coercion and pressure. He needs to get rid of his anxiety and leave his fears of being locked up again behind him.

Thursday night

I go out with some other kids. Tom had missed an earlier meeting we'd planned. When I see him later, he simply says, 'I'm sorry to have caused you trouble John.'

He's growing, clearly taking more reasonable risks; I feel that he wants and very much needs to keep our relationship moving.

There is a problem with kids on bikes in our area. The bike is almost irresistible to these children; the mythology, the power, the love of the chase, the speed, the exhilaration. A high percentage of police involvement with our kids revolves around the riding and registration of bikes. The kids need a safe, legally acceptable locality for riding them.

Friday

Tom is playing a 'come and chase me' game, alternating with 'I'm gonna show John I can really stand on my own feet.' I don't say much and head off for a quiet weekend.

Sunday

We're in the lounge room of the flat. Tom, Katy, and Tom's mother are watching T.V. I sit on the floor.

There's Tom, wanting to go somewhere, anywhere, using the whole atmosphere; his mother, blocking, fearing, wanting order; and me, caught wanting to talk to Tom, perhaps, or to do some reading with him. Tom could walk out leaving both of us, or speak obviously or sneakily in front of Katy about going out with me; and the outcome depends on what has happened earlier that day to all of us. For instance, has an argument taken place? Has Tom been at home or at school? What sorts of moods are John and Tom's mother in? His mother, wanting Tom at the flat, yet knowing his other wishes, is fearful of her son's perverse nature. Katy, knowing the scene, sucks up to her mother or to me or plays both of us off against Tom, baiting her brother or her mother or both.

As for me, I feel the walls coming in. I am wanting to maintain Tom's relationship with his family, yet to do this now I need to work with Tom alone. The problem is to stay or go, but if we go, where do we go? The pool room, the Coffee Shop or for a drive?

July

Tuesday, a week later

I don't see Tom for a few days.

Today Tom is with his mates at the back of the flats. When I arrive he races up expectantly to see me. During the evening he stays close and reads, talks and plays in a great burst of animation. I sense him moving forward.

He has a technique of flitting from one person to another, not always deliberately. It's another of his survival strategies and I think it's a destructive one. Yet how do I help him to see how superficial these contacts are? He has a genuine need for relationships of a more meaningful and continuing nature than the ones he establishes on this basis.

Wednesday

Tom is still being shunted between his own needs and the demands I am putting on him. It is clear there is a need to develop short-term programmes for him – whether at school, at home, or on trips – that will give him a sense of commitment in his relationships with others.

Wednesday, a week later

I am certain that an adult male's presence is necessary for a child's growth and maturation. Few people question the importance and function of the maternal role in a child's development. The role of the father is less clearly prescribed and valued, either in the literature of child development or in people's minds. It's my belief that a young child is an emerging human being, full of potential, who doesn't develop as fully without the physical presence of constant and secure female and male caring figures, whether they are the biological parents or not.

Would Tom Goodwood have been better off without his father, or were the traumas suffered worth their limited relationship? Are his problems the result of deprivation or of his father's treatment of him? Are 'bad' parents worse than no parents? Is one caring parent, in Tom's case, his mother, better than two warring, troubled ones? And what about the nature of the hurt inflicted on the child? These questions trouble me.

How can boys who have only fleetingly known an aggressive or violent father relate to other male authority figures? These boys often act according to the rules prescribed for mother–son relationships. They just don't know the ground rules for relating to an older man. Do they have to learn a new ritual?

Tom definitely needs a constant, older male in his life. Yet it is more than this. He *wants* his own male attachment figure. I wonder if one child's needs for their mother or their father are stronger than another's? I notice with all the fatherless boys I work with that they have a desperate need for a virile, male attachment figure. In a working-class area the male's role is heavily stereotyped and these boys need an acceptable male figure on which to model themselves.

Far more than all these things is the need for a loving environment. Last time Tom spent a night in Geelong he slept in a room by himself. He decided, despite some hesitancy, to overcome his fears. I was rather proud of him. He felt good, secure and safe in the bedroom, as it was part of a larger, accepting and caring setting. 'I feel at home here,' he said. These little changes are big breakthroughs.

Thursday

Tom is working well. He read a Jim Hunter book for

me last night. I must find some material that has simple language but at the same time is full of things that interest and spark off ideas in a fourteen-year-old boy; something that will maintain his interest without being patronizing.

He fluctuates, emotionally and intellectually, in his capacity to understand and interact with other human beings; yet there is some harmony in him now. No doubt he will have great confrontations and periods of regression in the future, but I doubt if he will fully stagnate again. Our relationship has given him a chance to develop his potential, to become what he wants to become within the framework of his working-class world. He can freely express himself and sort out his personal confusions without being hurt or destroyed by them.

The reading session is almost a breakthrough. Tom's work is expressive. He enjoys the learning situation and the feedback from people. There is real movement in his personality and I sense it springs from more than mere survival. Tom has a pushing, probing, testing animation.

Sunday night

Tom is caught between his mother, my coming and going, and the usual brother and sister love–hate struggle, and he blows up about minor things. He sits refusing to speak, then he argues with his mother and throws the birdcage to the floor in petulant anger. I take him into his bedroom and we stare hard into each other's eyes. At least he hasn't run away; he's here with me. He calms down and we talk gently; the feelings seem even stronger than before.

I believe for the first time he has found a loving relationship in which there is genuine, creative communication. When blocks occur, both Tom and I struggle to achieve an honest expression of our personal and mutual needs.

Monday night

Broken agreement. Tom is at Lee's place. I go there. Rejection. 'I'm not comin' with yuh.' Lee asks, 'Why should he go with yuh?'

I leave and go to Rosemary's, but I'm barred by Lee on my return and threatened with violence.

Lee says, 'I'll call the cops and put yuh in for trespass.' We avoid a physical confrontation. Tom sits behind Lee. Lee says, 'Shut up Tom and do what I say.' Tom, guilty, is not really able to play the old game with Lee as the boss. We leave distressed because we don't want this sort of battle. It would be disastrous for all of us.

Tuesday night

Tom is missing. Rosemary and I go out looking for him but we can't find him. I become increasingly full of fears and lost feelings. I wonder what to do: I can't behave like a cop, I don't want to invoke his mother's legal powers, I don't want him to stay with Lee, but above all I don't want him to feel I've abandoned him.

Wednesday night

Tom is found. He goes off again and is finally tracked down near the station. He is up on the roof of the fish shop. My feelings are ones of sheer despair. Lee and the kids have gathered around. There's laughter, an atmosphere of sneering gaiety, 'Will he jump?'

Tom's mother has turned up and is angry with Lee who threatens to bash her. Other kids are furiously riding their bikes round and round the fish shop. There's yelling, and angry voices. A mad, mad circus; it's a high-wire act with no safety net.

Tom suddenly stands up, high on the rooftop, a small frightened child against the city skyline.

'Shut up and stop arguin',' he yells.

Lee hovers around, caught in his role. Tom acts in a hostile way towards me. 'I'll come down, but he has to go first.'

'Sorry Tom, no blackmail.'

Neon lights flash in my eyes. I see the fragile boy on the roof and people behaving as if they're at a carnival.

As we talk he thaws out. Lee grows restless, realizing that he's losing his hold over Tom. What is Tom's susceptibility? Lee says to Rosemary, 'If he comes down he'll go with John and his mother.'

It's a raw power struggle: Lee symbolizes the old system; Rosemary and I represent the future.

Later, we go to the flat. We are all full of ambivalent feelings. I contemplate which way I should lead him now. What role am I in? Am I being restrictive, binding, perhaps ultimately destructive? Should I come or go? But if I stay, how should I handle it?

Tuesday

Tom, Rosemary and I are at Rosemary's place, Tom's playing with me, but I'm too defensive about Rosemary's mother's property to play hard. He grows frustrated, clashes with Rosemary, disappears briefly, but returns, saying, 'I'm sorry for causin' a scene.' He looks pensive, wondering possibly if this apology will be accepted.

We desperately need a place where we can really work these things through. As Rosemary says, 'You're always left to finish other people's mistakes with Tom.'

Yet his movement forward is real and sustained. His

self-awareness is stronger and growing and his self-esteem is showing signs of restoration. Earlier he wrote and spelt for me, enjoyed the exercise, and watched eagerly as I counted up the mistakes.

I think I'll get him writing. The time is right, he wants to learn and grow.

Thursday night

Tom is at home, belligerent, highly strung and abusive. Violence is impending, building up to a bust-up with his mother, another re-run of moments of the past.

His mother says, 'I've had enough . . . I'll slap your face if you keep going.'

'Try it and I'll kick yer 'ead in.'

His mother reddens. Tom tenses, tightens, clenches his fist. I break the bind, pick him up, throw him over my shoulder and leave, muttering, 'I'll see you later.'

We sit in the car. He sulks, tries to find the old pattern but fails, so snaps back to reality.

We talk. He says that when I was carrying him he tried to hit me, he aimed at the back of my head, gritted his teeth, shut his eyes, but couldn't do it.

Have I broken the shut-on/shut-off mechanism? Why does he surface with me? Why does he snap back to his emerging self?

I question the process, the mechanism, the encounter, the hold I have, the hold he has. Without our physical encounters the relationship suffocates.

Friday night

Another broken arrangement. I find Tom at the Harold Street flats. I challenge his broken agreement. 'I'm not makin' no more promises,' he says. I grab him, throw him in the car and drive to a deserted spot.

It's a raw encounter, no physical action, just words,

hostilities and anger. Tom grows quiet and pensive. I am terribly frustrated and hot. There's no physical scene, no release sequence for an hour or more.

We start to talk calmly. A different stage of his struggle is emerging: his problem of actually living with a caring person; how he should handle his own feelings in his interaction with me. These are the birth pangs, the pains he must conquer on the way to self-realization. The ambivalences, the lifestyle strategies of the past, the present relationship, the peer group pressure to return to the old behaviour, and my presence in the family setting must all be sorted out.

He talks straight to me, puts out a series of proposals about how he intends to tackle his problems and we talk about them.

I can feel Tom's struggle for some wholeness. How can I disarm his self-destructive behaviour and support his genuine forward movement?

I wonder why, at stressful moments, he cuts off, or tries to cut off, the key attachment figures in his life. Can there be no replacement for the loss of a parent? What is it about him that is so elusive? Is it his loss, his anxiety or his erratic behaviour? Is it something we haven't even considered? Will he ever risk real growth again? Even with a new, kind rider, a brutalized horse pulls and tosses its head as if expecting to be whipped and beaten.

More than humane re-conditioning is needed.

August

Sunday night

Tom is at a school camp. While he is away his mother talks honestly to me about her difficulties with him. I ask her if he sometimes reminds her of her husband.

'At times he seems to get all the attention . . . he turns his back on me and goes off with anyone handy . . . I find it hard to keep calm with him, I start yelling at him for what he's doing to me . . . I can't control him, yet he's still my son.'

Tuesday

Tom has an uninhibited love of fantasy, of children's stories, of films like *The Wizard of Oz*, and of innocent playful dialogue, when he is with Rosemary and me. His imagination was fired by a trip to Fairy Park near Werribee with me a while back. He showed interest in the various figures — Snow White, Little Red Riding Hood, Jack and the Beanstalk — and wanted to know the stories and fables about them. He is similarly fascinated by horror stories, ghost stories and movies, although a deeper mechanism is involved here, a type of sadistic or masochistic thing. Hardly anyone communicates with Tom in these unexplored areas. Perhaps they can't handle their own fantasies.

Wednesday

Tom's approach to his girl friends shows an innocence of life's destructiveness. He has no yardstick with which to understand and measure potential. He doesn't agree (even in mimicking me) with his mates' 'belt 'em if they deserve it' approach. He is genuinely searching for warmth and love. He once told me, 'I was nine when I first tried, but it wasn't big enough, so I had to wait a year. I got in on all the gang bangs from the next year. I used to go first because it was my girl friend we fucked.'

Thursday

Last night he didn't come as arranged. Tonight he was very late. We talk about why he acts as he does.

'Guess I do it because of the stuff that happened with me dad.'
'How?'
'Ah . . . some guy in the Home told me it.'
'What?'
'I'd been around women too long . . .'

Later he says 'I wouldn't accept me dad was gone, so I wouldn't read or write or do anythin' at school.'

Here it is. The stop–start thing, the really desperate need for some continuity.

'I just forget arrangements when I'm with me mates or doin' somethin'.' 'I'm really changin' yuh know, I don't have fits anymore. Kids can't get me to throw 'em. Yuh don't know what me friends are like at times, "Fuck this, fuck that."

'I'll write yuh some of the things I did in me past, like when I was in the Institution.'

He is still lying at times, though not with the same desperate cunning or abandon, and as the pattern has been partially broken, he is learning, slowly, to talk through the reasons for his lying and some self-realization is occurring.

We are also spending time on the inconsistencies of Tom's entrenched behaviour patterns. I am aware that everybody has moments of erratic behaviour; perhaps with a damaged person they just occur more often.

But I still want a basic honesty from him. I don't push him at times over his failure to keep his arrangements. At other moments when I sense no hidden hurts, I insist at all costs, that we work through the impasse. Tom's more friendly, erratic behaviour is a vast improvement on that of the boy I met last year, but there is still a long way to go.

Don't Push the River — Barry Stevens is right; yet, we are also in the business of breaking 'life scripts' as Eric Berne terms it.

Saturday

I am thinking about Tom, his girl friend and her father. I called to pick him up from the girl's house one day last week. He told her father that I pulled him out by the hair. I found this out one night when he didn't want me to meet her father.

'Why not?'
'He thinks yuh don't treat me right.'
'Uh . . . um . . . er?'
'He thought yuh pulled me out by me hair the other night.'

I am left speechless.

Rosemary says the girl friend's father might be like Tom's. He is a small, overweight man, with an obvious grudge against the world. I don't feel happy in his company.

There is some deep vulnerability in Tom, some propensity for relationships of a potentially dangerous kind. Am I being over-protective? I want him moving outwards, meeting new people, seeing new scenes. What should I do? I must try to keep the forward momentum, but at the same time, carefully steer him away from potential binds and dead ends.

Monday

After a good weekend, he plays intensely with me, he's all over me, pulling, shoving, rubbing, punching me with increasing power, becoming almost frantic. I have to draw back from him; I sense an explosion coming on. I'm not sure what causes this intensity nor whether I can control it.

When he calms down, we talk and he tells me, as he often does, about his father.

'One night he brought us home a great big bag of popcorn. I knocked a bit of it over and he went berko and kicked me round the room.'

I remind him about the night he was playing softly with Katy. She did some minor thing that annoyed him. A shadow crossed his face, he turned and knocked her away and then kicked her forcefully in the back.

School holidays

Tom's grandfather has died. His mother goes to the funeral.

We spend the next five days in Geelong. They are crucial days in our relationship. We work out a practical agreement for third term, covering nights out, weekend arrangements, his rights and the rights of others. He starts to do little things like clean his teeth, make his bed, help me wash the car and discuss arrangements for following days. He is beginning to take account of small human differences.

The agreement is an attempt to place known clearcut structures around his existence. It aims to give him security to help him to understand other people's expectations of him and to accept the consequences of his actions.

Rosemary, Tom and I spend an exciting afternoon at the You Yangs. Tom plays with Rosemary's young puppy. They chase each other around in circles, frollicking, jumping and racing madly off into the distance, both enjoying their game.

That night he asks, 'Will yuh do some work with me John?' We centre on our trip earlier that day. He wants me to write up what we have done, 'Yuh write real good. Go on, do it just this time.' I ask him to write it up with me.

He may not read or write like a fourteen-year-old, yet he feels and thinks like a sensitive young man. It is a rare, exhilarating experience to see the work he produces for me. Tom's abilities rarely emerge, not even at the Annexe, where he still acts as a boy who has no real talent. Perhaps it is only when he's with me that he feels safe enough to show his sensitivity.

After the death of her father, Mrs Goodwood is very vulnerable. She fluctuates between her idealization of him, saying, 'What a wonderful father he has been. I don't know what I'll do without him' and her more realistic assessment, commenting, 'You know, he never really cared about my mum.'

Tom and his mother start to argue. They are at cross purposes.

'What does he care,' she says, 'his grandfather really cared about him . . . he acts mean when I'm upset.'

Tom says, 'Leave me alone . . . I care, only leave me alone.'

With me, he plays and plays and plays. There have been three or four tearful moments every couple of days, yet we talk and work them out. We talk about people, things, feelings. 'Why I pushed people . . . I don't know . . . what I wanted from yuh . . . the old game, me mates still play it all the time.'

I have a couple of deep discussions with his mother.

'I fight with him when he's here, yet it's funny, when he's not here I miss him.'

Thursday
In the past few days Tom has started to work into a daily routine. I leave him at home saying, 'See how things go. I'll see you in a couple of days.'

Friday
I'm having a quiet night down in Geelong by myself.

There is something about Tom I want to understand. His problems seem to originate in his lack of parental care, in the accumulation of traumas (especially the scenes with his father, the Institution and the school defeats). Yet his loss is that he has never been given any ordinary affection and love in his life.

The dynamic and form of human change are as diverse as human difference itself. They are always individualistic. You may be accurate in classifying a person ninety-nine per cent of the time, yet miss that one possibility for change.

My thoughts are interrupted. Rosemary is on the phone. She says she's just spent a remarkable hour at the Goodwoods'. Mrs Goodwood and the children are behaving like a healthy, happy family unit. Tom's mother is amazed at the change in him, the little everyday things he now does. While he shows flashes of temper, he feels no need to hit out. Tom's mother says his clothes are too tight for him — he put on some weight in Geelong where he ate steak, eggs and drank some milk and orange juice. Before that he had only eaten tinned food, meat pies and that sort of 'plastic' food. His face is now full, open and happy.

September

Sunday

Tom spent the remaining days of the holidays with his family. He didn't come home one night and we talked about it later. 'I shut the consequences out of me mind, yuh don't think about what follows. I could have come home if I'd wanted to.'

We kept our agreement; he lost his following weekend night out. There was a calm acceptance of this.

I now see the real signs of continuity in his life. He feels and stretches the very first security he has known with acceptance and understanding. He feels safe to develop his own personality. His emergence is not partial, there is a growing wholeness about him.

Tuesday night

After two days back at school Tom shows signs of distress, hostility and anxiety. He feels trapped in the old school environment. The open, alert face he displayed a few days ago is becoming lined with frustration, worry and tension.

'Why do they keep pushin' me? . . . I get the blame for everythin' that happens . . . I don't understand a lot of the work and the teachers won't help me.'

A child who is trying to break a behaviour pattern that has been forced upon him requires the support of teachers likewise prepared to dispense with stereotypes and rigid patterns of behaviour.

He wants to learn. He wrote and spelt tonight. Initially he was tight and resistant, shrugging his shoulders, feigning boredom. I asked him what the problem was.

'I dunno.'

'Now, don't give me any of that crap, what's bugging you?'

'School's givin' me the shits.'

We talk about it, consider how to stop screwing up so tight, how to minimize unnecessary tensions; and he opens up and works with zest and skill. I think about the labels that are hung on kids. Tom has been given many derogatory ones. Somehow I must help him to cope with the stress they place on him and encourage him to struggle to reject them.

I go home and listen to Jimmy Buffet's 'A1A' L.P.,

side two, a song called 'A Pirate Looks at Forty'. His songs of the sea soak into me and revive me when nothing else works. It is my nourishment and I keep it for late at night when I need to be alone, it transports me into the ebb and flow of the sea. I share most of my intimate moments with other people, yet my music is my own.

During my childhood I grew to love the sea. I would walk for hours on the beach when the pressures of growing up threatened to disintegrate my fragile self-esteem. To push out into the rolling surf and meet its onslaught with all the force I could muster was my therapy. I still love to roam on gusty, blowy days on deserted, sandy surf beaches.

Wednesday night

Tom's mother is happy and at ease, the children play calmly together. Recently she has shown signs of genuine relaxation with her children. She was worried about Katy and her school work, but didn't want to have an argument, so she asked me to talk to her. 'She won't speak to many people, but she likes talking about things with you.'

The members of the family are struggling so hard to get on with each other now; there is even a willingness to risk showing some of their deeper needs and individuality.

Tom's mother told me that her sister, who helps out at the technical school, was talking to Mary Loxley. Mary said she'd seen Tom one afternoon late last term, and commented on how different he was. 'He wasn't as nervous and jerky as he used to be. There was a quiet confidence about his movements . . . and he was courteous and thoughtful.' Tom's mother received really positive feedback from this communication.

She went on to talk about Tom's father. 'He got to

hate Tom ... if I bought him a new pair of shoes he had to have a new pair as well ... he'd be real good and take Tom camping with him, then he would suddenly turn on him — at times he'd just knock him out of the way.'

Thursday

Tom is wrestling with me in a rollicking, carefree way, giving and taking. Somehow, I sense he is in a missed stage of his development. He gets stronger and harder. I push back just as hard. He laughs and his eyes sparkle.

'I'm gonna give it to yuh real good, yuh suck.'

There's a probing, animated expression on his face.

'If you do, I'm going to carry you out into the rain.' He was playing in shorts and tee-shirt.

'Yeah?' He punched me with deliberation and controlled hardness, then fixed me with a cold stare and raised his eyebrows. I throw him over my shoulder and carry him out and do a circuit of the flats in the light, drizzling rain. He giggles, complains, fights, and becomes stern, 'Don't be so bloody stupid John ... it's cold.' He sulks for a few moments when we go back inside, then turns and looks at me with a dawning understanding. All the fragmented aspects of Tom's past are coming together and making his behaviour more comprehensible to himself and other people.

Wednesday night

Late again. Tom is in great turmoil over his erratic behaviour. He seems to want to make some deep statement, yet is unable to reach into his own distress. He's putting his whole being before me, 'Help me, do somethin' with me, find the things that make me act as I do.'

We sit overlooking the dark night sea. Tom breathes

more quickly than before, struggling to relieve himself of some desperate, ever present burden, caught before an eruption; fearful, yet strong enough to risk the deluge.

'I'm scared, I can't stop meself, I can't stand meself at times.'

He starts to shake, to heave for air, as if he is bursting to break clear of some strangling hold.

'I keep seein' this face all the time.'

'Whose face?'

'The boy's I was in the Institution with.'

'What's it like?'

'I can't.' He is almost vomiting with effort. 'I can't . . .'

'Tell me!'

'It's all screwed up and tight.' He screws up tight, every muscle hardens. 'And he just looks at yuh, he can't speak, he won't, he just stares, and stares and stares and . . . he grabs yuh tighter and tighter.' He contorts his body, struggles and grasps out for support. I hold him tight, my arms around his shoulders.

'Go on Tom, tell me how he looks at you.'

'I can't, I see him all the time. When I go to bed I see his face.' Tom is crying and struggling forward now. 'He used to touch me. I couldn't stand it, he'd grab me tighter. I told him not to but he just kept goin' harder and harder. I wanted me mum to come, or especially me dad, but they never did. The people in the Home wouldn't listen to me. They said it was my fault for runnin' away and I had to stay with him in that room every night. He'd throw fits and go mad.'

'What did you do?'

'I'd sit in the corner and hope he wouldn't see me and he'd just look and look at me.'

Tom breaks down, shaking with fear. I hold him up and say. 'Tell me about his eyes Tom.'

'They are all wide open, always wide open and mad, he'd just stare at the walls for hours.'

'Did you think you'd go like him?'

Clearer, strong now, 'Yeah, I thought I'd go like he was. I've always been scared of bein' like that meself after I got out of the Home. I couldn't stand anyone to touch me. I'd just go tight and crazy like he did. I swore I'd never speak to adults after I got out . . . never, anyone.'

His exhaustion afterwards was a positive sign, but why wasn't this unearthed earlier, by someone, anyone?

Thursday

I thought it would help Tom to go through this whole experience in detail. We sat down together to put it all on paper and this is what came out.

> First time I went into the Institution I was all right, but I wouldn't speak to anyone. Then I went to court. I was put into the open section. I ran away. Then I was made a ward of the state. I was put in Northside, the locked up section of Baltara, for four weeks. After this time I ran away from the open section, because I wanted to be home. This time I was put for another month in Northside. I was in with a mentally disturbed kid. He wouldn't speak or eat for a while, then he started having fits, like busting things up, trying to get out. I used to just sit in the corner and watch. I was scared to do anything because somebody like that could kill you. He looked like he was always in agony. His face was always screwed up, his eyes were wide open. After I came home I had nightmares about him. I was scared of the dark, of the night coming, of going to sleep, of his face and of him. I was scared he might throw a fit and kill me. I thought he'd come and get me. I just see his face. I'd go

to bed and see his face all screwed up, trying to get out, his screwed up, wrinkled face. All the time he was tight. He had real wide eyes, his mouth was always kept tight, all his muscles were as tight as they could be. I used to get tight when he moved. I was scared of him. I couldn't sleep much. All night I'd sit up on the bed. I was scared to go to sleep; I still was when I came out. He used to grab my hands and squeeze them like he wanted help or something. People touched me and I tensed up. I was always up in the corner away from him. I was scared of him. He'd grab me and squeeze my hands real tight, as hard as he could, his eyes just staring at the wall. I always thought of him touching my hands. I just tensed a little harder each time, until I got as hard as I could.

Sometimes I try to reach deep inside Tom and experience life as he does. Of course I can't really do it, yet something in me has to take heed of his pulsebeat and be moved by the same urges that are moving him.

What did he go through in the experiences mapped out in the previous pages?

An eleven-year-old boy locked in a strange, cold room. He takes in the signals from his body. He feels cold; he sees everything grey and the place smells so antiseptic. Everything is sterile and bleak; nothing that you touch or feel or see or smell is familiar. There's no one around: no father, no mother, no friend, no protector. He thinks of escape.'I'll do this . . . I'll wait until . . . I'll get out through the . . .' Real despair mounts inside him, waves of nausea pass over him, he has moments when he longs for safety, then feels bitterness and anger at his mother for letting them take him. 'Why, why?' He twists and tightens his body, hatred for her surging through him 'I'll make her suffer.'

He is caught between the need to close off, to become tough so he can survive and the despair he feels, and his need as a small boy to express the pain and hurt. How does he make sense of it all? His being is in too much turmoil to be untangled by logic. He survives, but how? In there, it's a life and death struggle. To survive he must take over just about anything.

He shuffles into the half dark room, the door is shut behind him by an attendant. He looks around, slowly, cautiously, the room feels hostile: the regimented, cold walls, the windows with bars, the old bunked beds. Then he sees the face. There's something wrong with it. He shivers violently. Then some fascination makes him look again. He looks at the face, the wide-opened staring eyes, the tight mouth and the pale, wooden cheekbones. A deep, sickening fear rises from the pit of his stomach.

'I've got to get out. Help, somebody, take me out of here.' He bangs against the door, harder and harder, yelling as loud as he can, 'Help me, let me out.' Of course, no one comes. They can hear, he knows that, but no one comes. They've put you in here, your mother has left you here.

Suddenly a cold hand presses against his arm. He jumps back. The other face just stares, he feels the tightening grip on his arm. Cold terror. 'Get away from me, get away.' No reply, only the wide, open eyes, the shaking grip on his arm. The sound of teeth grinding, the red blotches on the white, pallid skin. He withdraws stiffly, against the wall; the other boy just stares through him. Why won't he speak? A deep knot ties inside his gut; his fear, 'I'll go like that.' As the other boy starts to have his fits and it gets darker, he thinks, 'Nobody cares about me.' He crouches smaller and smaller, knowing there is no point in shouting or yelling, yet wanting to talk about the other boy. He begins to think it's his fault for running away. The faces, the cold, rigid bodies of the people in charge flash through his mind. 'Help me, help me!' No one comes. He starts to clench his teeth, he sits in the corner and stares at the wall. The other boy grabs him and presses him tighter and tighter, leaving dark bruises. The other boy hits the walls with his hands and kicks wildly at the beds. He tightens his body defensively, knowing the boy could kill him.

'I've got to get out, can't, got to get out, can't . . . can't tell anyone . . . they won't listen . . . won't talk.' The other face, those eyes, those hands; just there, all the time.

'I can't stand it, help me, someone help me . . .' He grits his teeth harder, won't look at anything, stares at nothing, doesn't care, shuts off.

After a month Tom was taken out of this section.

'I hope you've learnt about running away Tom,' the Superintendent said, somewhat puzzled by the faraway look in the boy's eyes and somewhat repelled by the rigidity and tightness of the boy's face and movements. And the clenched teeth worried him. 'Something wrong with this boy,' he thought, 'must get one of my psychologists on to it, should have picked it up before.' And the eyes, buried, glassy, unreachable, 'I think this boy could be dangerous for other boys to be with, don't like the look in his eyes.'

Somewhere beneath lies a boy.

Friday

What a week! Since the catharsis Tom experienced in telling me of his terrifying month in the Home he seems to have been freed from a great burden. I think he will be able to make great advances now that his trauma has been uncovered. He now knows that there are people who care for him and who will help him face his worst moments and he radiates a new self-confidence.

I keep him going in what is seen by some as a dictatorial fashion. We work every night on some reading, writing or basic maths problem. He eagerly absorbs new facts and keeps asking, 'Am I goin' all right?'

At the Annexe he is working well, although he still tends to clam up when he encounters a new situation. I think the teachers there, particularly the middle-class ones, are wary of him. He still gives people the feeling they should keep their distance.

At home things are changing for the better. I have a meal with the family at least once a week; his mother leaves me to handle the heavy, sometimes physical scenes, and she is more at ease with him. I can now talk with her honestly and directly and Tom is starting to do little things in the home for her like asking her how she feels, washing the dishes, playing with his sister, and cleaning up after his shower.

We must keep this process going. We are only a breath away from Tom being able to handle his own life, though he still needs another year at the Annexe to catch up on his lost years of education.

I have been placed in a position where he *expects* me to demand things of him, and to show my anger if he doesn't keep his promises. By this time next year our whole relationship of intense, daily, face-to-face involvement will have been going on for nearly three years. How many other children require the same time, concern and analysis? I don't think anything worthwhile and lasting can be achieved in any less time.

For instance, there is a seventeen-year-old boy, Sammy who was charged with rape and resisting arrest with a gun and a knife last week. He had accidentally shot his father when he was about seven years old. He could have received profound help then, or later on when he was obviously a disturbed, unhappy, unsuccessful schoolboy at Williamstown Tech. But help came too late, he ran out of time. I don't think much can be done to help Sammy now.

A couple of Saturdays back he and his mates had had too much to drink and I came across him kicking another boy's face in. The other boy lay semi-conscious on the ground and he was attacking him with great viciousness. I intervened, threw Sammy out of the way, and carted the wounded boy off to the Newport Hospital. Tom was with me; Sammy had been a friend of his.

Later in the car, Tom asked me, 'Why didn't yuh have a talk to Sammy and stop him from doin' it again? He'd take notice of yuh.' Who knows? Perhaps he could have been helped, though I think not.

Perhaps you can only have this demanding and intense relationship with someone you feel a deep affection for; care and understanding can be given to everyone, yet I find myself unable to relate to every hurt child I meet with the same gusto. I am certain that a boy like Sammy, to become healthy, needs his own special person to care for him, to go into his corner at times and work through his problems with him. I could help Sammy, but I doubt if I could ever deeply affect him. There have to be caring people in the community who can meet these kids on their own terms.

The Williamstown town planner rang to say we could have two or three rooms of an old library which had been taken over by the council for welfare services if we wanted them, and if we could persuade the Education Department to give us a grant. The place is central and suitable for our type of work.

Increasingly, I see the importance of setting up a small, close-knit environment for those children who are close to destruction. This old library could be the answer. Our work needs to be intimate and face-to-face, carried out somewhere that is accessible to the local schools, troubled parents and interested outsiders.

October

Sunday

The Goodwoods go to visit Tom's aunt, Toni, who lives in Werribee. Mrs Goodwood has remained close friends with her husband's sister, even during the break up of her marriage.

'We used to see each other all the time. Now we meet a couple of times a year. It's our turn to visit them this year and as Tom's been so good I thought we'd all go. He used to get on real good with Doug, his cousin. I didn't realize that their girl's wedding (so far her voice was clear and calm, now it grows tight and anxious) is next Saturday. Toni invited us to the older girl's but my husband Jim wasn't asked. This was before we were divorced. He was real drunk and stupid at the time. He'd just been in for stealing a car. He got real mad and gatecrashed the reception and he ended up giving his mum a black eye. Toni said she didn't know what to do.

'Jim's back with his mum and dad again. Toni's heard he's drinking a lot and she's afraid if he's not invited to the wedding he'll take it out on them. When she asked us if we wanted to go, Tom was there, and looked real strained when she mentioned his dad's name. She said they'd have a lot of large fellas there if Jim got drunk and turned nasty, but I didn't know what to say; I don't want my children to think we should be scared of him but I'm still frightened he'll take it out on Tom if he gets into one of his moods. I said I'd talk to you about it.'

We talk it over and she decides not to go. Then we go on discussing Tom's progress.

'I'm really happy with the kids now . . . Tom's talking to me, he stays around the flats and does what you tell him . . . we have good meals when you come down. He comes straight home and waits to do his work with you. I don't want to lose it now.'

Wednesday

I want to take another look at the cathartic sessions we had last week. They all appear to have a similar dynamic; first a minor let-down, then my insistence on an explanation, followed by Tom's silence. The more I try to get him to talk it out the more stubborn he becomes.

It's a time of silent, seething hostility, unbearable tension. Eventually my persistence wins through. He talks and the tension is relaxed. My probing is unearthing hidden traumas that have been nagging away at him one by one. Each must be brought to the surface and worked out of his system. Our mutual trust creates a fertile atmosphere for this process. Tom now has a safe base from which he can reach out into the world and confront his own inner demons. Up to now, he couldn't risk these self-explorations. He was living in a nightmarish world. He isolated and repressed the pain, which made his life unbearable, into his subconscious but this left him deeply confused and anxious.

His experiences in the Institution badly frightened him. He deliberately refused to learn to read or write. He would not allow human closeness — his physical and mental worlds were unsafe and in this turmoil he was unable to develop his learning capacity.

How could he get out of this nightmare? He needed a trusted, dependable older person, who could stand with him and look his monsters in the face and not freeze with fear. Our relationship has provided this safe space and safe time in which to unearth, understand and exorcize these terrifying traumas of his past.

Tom has already seen and experienced his father's violence to his mother and himself. This scarred his ability to be receptive to love and affection. The repercussions from this violence around him so disorientated his whole growing process that he was unable to work out who he was, where he was, or what real human relationships he wanted.

The month that he spent encaged with the other desperate child in Baltara in mounting shock and horror destroyed any trust he may have had in life or people. He took over the other child's symptoms to survive. He became the other child. It made him almost totally unable to cope with the outside world. He couldn't manage his own confused feelings. There was no safety anywhere. What seemed to be good, loving and responsive could turn out hateful and self-destructive. How could he separate one message from another? A crazy jumble of feelings and messages came into being. He was in total confusion.

I had a dream earlier this term, in which I was unable to discriminate between friends and foes. I remember being in Payne's office at the Williamstown Tech. We were arguing, probably about how to deal with problem kids. I felt cornered, anxious and totally inadequate. Payne was huge and full of overbearing confidence. Just as I blew my cool and started to yell and advance on Payne, I lost my conceptual clearness. I couldn't make out the face before me. Then to my horror I saw Tom's face, Peter's face, Tony's face, all with Payne's expression and bearing. I felt stupid — this must be a different day, I thought — yet the same words and feelings came from these other faces, as if the earlier conversation was this conversation, as if Payne's face was their face, his being was their being. I tossed and struggled to comprehend the differences, that something was wrong, evidently some strange thing had happened. During this mental struggle I lost my focus and then became aware of a different setting. The feeling, the battle, the words were the same, only this time I was in court, on trial, before a large group of hooded people, some small, some large in appearance. I knew the small frames belong to my kids, so I furiously started to work out which legs and arms and sizes were Tom's, Lee's, Sammy's and so on. It became a mad panic. Nobody responded to my questions. I was unable to work things out.

Obviously the dream had to do with my own deepest fears; they revolved around the problem of trust: who are your real friends, do people all wear the same mask?

Tom in his everyday dealings with people was in this untrusting, unknowing, fearful situation. His human development was in turmoil. He has had experiences that have produced dehumanizing, traumatic arrests in his personality. An almost inevitable loss of trust in life has left him insecure and damaged.

In my dream I was unable to distinguish friend from foe and I feared the worst: deep down they were all the same. Tom's early experiences left him uncertain and self-doubting. During the month he spent locked up in Beltara, the whole structure of things collapsed. He became what he had to in order to survive. It has given me new insight, knowing that he still sees the other boy's contorted face, that he sweats as he feels the tightening hands on his body and that he senses the protruding, wide-eyed staring face looking right into him.

'Yuh think yuh'll go nuts like him after a while . . . nobody to help yuh . . . nobody cared, I thought I was no good, just rubbish to kick around . . .'

Wednesday night, a week later

Tom told me tonight that Duncan had been arrested and charged with murder.

I got to know Duncan through Rosemary at the Coffee Shop. He is one of the most vulnerable, most tender, yet cruellest kids I have ever known. I picked him up off the street once when he was blind drunk.

He beat up young boys in the toilets at the Coffee Shop. Tom and the other younger boys were frightened of something in him. Yet he writes songs for his girl friends, he protects Rosemary from any threat to her work with children. If anyone had touched or harmed her, God help them.

He told me one night, when drunk and beaten up, 'I'm no good, I'll spend the rest of me life in jail.'

He is a basic loner in life, so the kids he has beaten in individual fights often get together and attack him in a mob, usually when he is drunk and least able to defend himself. He cannot resist showing off in front of people. I knew there was real violence in him but Rosemary and I couldn't work it through. He is seventeen and time has run out for him.

November

Monday

This time I am going to write consciously and selectively about my own role. I recognize the fact that we all have our own emotional cycles. Most decidedly, a lot of the tension and perception of things comes directly from the state and stage of this cycle. Like most teachers I have an absorption rate and a tolerance pattern to do with my own reactions to noise, stress and ugliness. On some days I want stillness, quietness and calm; on others I need noise, animation and participation.

On days when I feel irritable, for no apparent reason, I find fault with Tom in damaging, unproductive ways. I focus on his agitations, his uncertainties, and on the noise and restlessness of his being. Once I am in a mood like this it is easy to see, hear and feel, the negative vibrations of other people, regardless of their actual behaviour. I seem determined to take them and use them as a whipping-post for my own straight-out satisfaction.

I was tired, feeling engulfed and lethargic, one night earlier this week. I hadn't liked school that day, was desperately tired of its confines, screwed up and nervy.

Tom on the other hand, was fine, relaxed, demanding and playful, I wasn't sure what I wanted to do: to stay, to go, to work, to play. I hung around, limp and cranky. He noticed the irritability I displayed on the surface and had the good sense not to provoke me. Nothing blew up. I just left as I came, uncertain and lethargic.

What is this terrible lethargy? I'm sure everyone suffers from it — the uncertain, restless, listless, shifts of feeling about their lives. It fosters indifference to one's self and to others and can make one extremely self-centred and difficult to get along with.

What is my situation with the Education Department? Months have gone by and I have heard nothing. I have rung the Department of Technical Administration and no one suitable is available to talk to me. I have written to them and received no reply.

Eventually I go in to the Technical Branch and discuss my future with a very senior person there. He says to me, 'I'm a politician more than anything else in my work. I say one thing to you behind the Department's closed doors about promises made to you or other people but if you quote me outside I'll call you a liar in public with all the force and status I can muster.'

This worries me greatly and casts a shadow over my work in Williamstown.

Tuesday

I heard yesterday that an Inspector will be out at Werribee Tech. to see me. I await this with real anticipation. He arrives. I am called in by the school Principal who knows nothing of my work last year, of my continuing involvement in Williamstown, or of my commitment to the kids there. We sit, the three of us, in the Principal's office. The Inspector looks down, I wait anxiously for some word, but it is the Principal who speaks.

'Fred and I have talked over your situation and we both agree that although we recognize the worth of what you are doing, there is just no way you can, at present, work full-time or part-time in the way you want to. The system hasn't any room for it, and there is no way it can foreseeably be done.'

I tell them then of the promise made to me last year. Their faces harden. I feel betrayed, disorientated and lost.

Wednesday

I discuss the Inspector's visit with my American friend and fellow humanities teacher.

She says, 'I know it, I saw it when I was working within the Catholic orders. They all do the same thing, shutting off doors that are different each time.'

I have been unable to reconcile the empathy expressed with my work and the complete refusal to honour past agreements that would allow it to continue. There is a book, really a manual of these things, written by Herbert Kohl, called *Half the House* that states it all.

He writes about a woman who was trying to keep her work with disturbed children going. She approached the local superintendent. 'She knew the superintendent's techniques for avoiding conflict or decisions. She had seen other people charmed or seduced into forgetting the political issues; she saw other people's egos tripped by false sympathy, but she felt immune. She knew that the superintendent was her enemy in the sense that he was willing to eliminate her programme, but she couldn't reconcile his manner with the role of an opponent.'

Thursday

I think I am seeing Tom's problems clearly now. Although there are still elusive, unexplored aspects, my understanding of his behaviour feels right. Tom is what he is as a result of irreconcilable forces within his environment, his family, his school life and his social existence. He has experienced erratic human caring, intermingled with physical punishments and brutal rejection. I often think of him as I first knew him. He was rarely at home, rarely, to my knowledge, participating in normal mother–son relationships. Mrs Goodwood cared for her son. He wanted to receive and give back natural affection, yet neither of them knew how to handle their own confused feelings.

At school, primary and technical, he was hit, abused and humiliated. 'They used to hit me almost every day in state school, I got the cuts for anythin' at all . . . at the time me dad left us I got into real trouble with the teachers because I wouldn't do any work. I used to get sent to the office all the time to get the strap . . . almost every day I got it for somethin' . . . me first day at the Tech. Payne gave me six for smokin' and not givin' me cigs to him . . . in me first year there and before I met yuh, I got it for smokin', for not bein' in class, for fightin', for waggin' . . . they used to hit me harder across the finger tips and wrists and I used to get real mad . . . yuh know they'd hit yuh and I'd always go and feel sorry for meself and sit in the toilets each time they hit me . . . I'd sit there all by meself and just get tighter and tighter and I'd wanna kill people . . . I'd hate gettin' in closed rooms after that . . . they'd just beat the hell out of yuh, they knew yuh couldn't do nothin' about it . . .'

Late Friday night

Another hard night at the Coffee Shop. Rosemary and I have a quiet chat in the early hours of the morning. Then we go for a walk along the dark, grassy foreshore near her mother's place. The waves absorb our deepest anxieties. The sky and wind calm our discontented minds. We walk for hours, feeling, smelling, absorbing nature around us. It has become our ritual for the release of tension. When you stand on the rocks near the water and look out to the hazy, purple and silvery horizon it's as if there's a magnet slowly pulling your body, rocking backwards and forwards.

We share and exchange our work and troubles. They are the same thing in the end. Difficult childhoods, a hostile world, runs of bad luck, young human beings ill-prepared for the struggle to survive. We talk about the mad chaos found in our kids' lives and about a specific child's trauma; how to untie the knots and rebuild the child's dignity.

We talk haphazardly of our own past, our families and friends and of our experiences that have left scars and wounds. We come across our own dreams of betrayal and terror and desertion, and those of our children and we try to piece them all together and find their universal symbols.

Our conversation brings to light the questions we both have about our work: how do children's deepest fears affect them in their growing years? What is the price they pay for their understanding of what is happening to them? What are the ways adults can drive children crazy by disordering their expectations so completely that they become dumbstruck?

We talk about fear and its impact on insecure children. It is very real to them and won't leave them alone. Where does a child turn when there is no loving, caring adult around? Children respond to fear with physical darts of pain and anguish. It can physically paralyse and control them day and night. The deeper the fear, the closer to death the child becomes. If the child is dependent upon some specific protection that is suddenly withdrawn, the fear can be quite overwhelming.

Stress is a natural part of animal and human life and it is encountered daily. But how many of our kids have been destroyed by stress because of their inability to cope with it unaided? Rosemary and I fear the enormous casualty rate among the kids because of this deprivation.

Monday

Payne, the teacher who physically and emotionally abused so many of the troubled boys at Williamstown Tech., is now in charge of school counselling. Is his appointment a deliberate act on behalf of the Education Department or is it just a complete farce?

Let me put it on the line here. I believe that Payne should be excluded from any teaching or counselling situation. If he stays in the Department and gains promotion it is a massive indictment of those individuals who run the schools. Those in charge must carry the responsibility for giving people like Payne licence to systematically destroy unprotected, already damaged children. This may be laughed at or shrugged off by those responsible for this situation but what I want them to know is this: the day of the 'cover-up' is over.

As for all those teachers, psychologists and parents who support this by their apathy or lack of concern and who refuse to rid the schools of the child bashers and soul murderers, they carry with them the same responsibility as those who went along with slavery, child labour and the subjugation of women. They are, to put it simply, 'gutless wonders'.

Tuesday

Tom missed an appointment last night. Today he says, 'I'm sorry John.'

Later, he sits quietly, wishing to please me. We talk for a short time. The pressure is on both of us now to keep our relationship going. Tom has been used to erratic and superficial contact with the people in his life. Our relationship exerts a new, and at times disturbing, pressure on him. It would probably be easier for him if I were slightly removed from his day-to-day situation — a sort of benevolent uncle figure — but I feel he has to cope with our regular sessions together as this is the only way for us to achieve progress.

His mother is still under great pressure. I really feel for her struggle to be more of a loving mother. She said tonight, 'You're the only person he's ever really taken notice of. You're the only man he's ever respected and looked up to, the only man he's ever let handle him with kindness and anger.'

I would like to help her reach a position where she can feel some sense of achievement with her son while I work on the conflicts.

Tom has yet to develop the ability to stand up to pressure. As in the past, in any moment of crisis or distress he reverts to his old pattern of withdrawal and abrupt assertiveness. The hardest thing is for him to resist the call back to his old mates and their way of life.

Tom also finds it hard to live with my constant pressure. He is struggling to take some control of his own life. I can't protect him too much or demand too much from him. He is wrestling to free the emerging Tom Goodwood from the old games, the old defences and the old roles he was forced to construct to survive. His battle is between the past fragmented, broken self and the emerging, but still very vulnerable one.

Thursday

We are really moving in the basic learning areas now. Tom is feeling the power of manipulation over words, numbers and other common, social symbols. Up until a few weeks back, he couldn't conceptualize 'two in to six' or 'four times four'. He did not possess the everyday skills so necessary to maintain any self-esteem.

In order to survive he constructs an alternative self-image, that of the tough, male-orientated bikie. He often says, 'What's these other things to me anyway', when he feels rejected and socially unacceptable.

Rosemary points out that he has not one object of value, no lasting symbols, no happy personal memories. He is endlessly on the move between people and objects, constantly reminded of his worthlessness, weaknesses and stupidities. He simply hasn't developed the skills to survive in our competitive society.

It's not surprising that Tom has never developed any feelings of self-respect. He was belted by his father, his teachers and the cops and then left to fend for himself in a world he could not comprehend. As he grew older this all intensified and he concluded that this was the way that life was going to be. Hence he has no yardstick for measuring other people's responses. He's developed no real capacity to order his own behaviour in terms of social norms and demands. At school, with his peer group, facing the fabric of social customs, he can only use basic, inept tactics. His responses are fragmented. He only knows his old self-destructive pattern of behaviour. This leads finally to a mental and physical stunting of his growth. At times he would reach a state of such inner turmoil that he would physically curl up into a ball in an attempt to return to the embryonic state.

Because of all these things, and their continual reinforcement, he had become almost totally narcissistic and self-centred. How could he make himself somebody in his own eyes?

I find this a most important area. The question to be asked about a boy like Tom is: when and how does he think of himself as a hero?

Wednesday morning

As a small boy I went to the paddocks with my father to hunt rabbits. He carried a double-barrelled shotgun, and I always walked behind him. We had a fox terrier. I am reminded of this as I sit at my desk this morning. The class has work to complete. I rarely sit at the teacher's desk, yet I do so this morning so I can look from the raised platform across the flat paddocks of Werribee, beyond the school. The yellowy brown grass stretches out to the horizon. The sun feels warm through the window glass and suddenly I find myself thinking back on a day in my own childhood.

The sky is blue above. Magpies are sitting on old fence posts. The grass is high and dry. I follow along down the creek bed with a warm breeze blowing loose dust into my face. There is no water; the long summer dried up the last pools weeks ago. I am looking up at the sky following the white cockatoos against the blue expanse.

Bang! Then another bang. I run full of new energy to see what's happening. My father stands there; his gun is open and there's smoke coming out. The foxie is barking furiously at a bush.

'Think I got him,' my father says, 'he was probably knocked over into the bush.'

I run up, expected to find an object lying still, covered with fluffy fur. I can't find it. The dog barks louder. I turn and freeze. Two real eyes stare up at me. Bloodshot eyeballs. I feel sick, terror-struck. The rabbit is whimpering, shaking; blood is running from its nose. I feel sick and want to run home to my mother. The rabbit tries to move, the dog is running around it. I see its eyes. Its eyes stay with me, rivet me to the spot and my feet won't move.

My father ambles up and says, 'Didn't quite shoot it dead, don't like to leave them like this.' He picks up the rabbit, its eyes almost pop out and it squeals loudly and horribly, and then drops limp to the ground. 'It's better to put it out of its misery,' he says to me.

Today I can still see the real blood-shot eyes of a hurt, trapped creature. Those eyes, almost human and childlike, have haunted me for years. I saw the same expression later when I got to know Tom and lived through his sieges. Like the rabbit, he would crouch in a corner, waiting for the final blow to come.

Wednesday night

The thing that makes man the most devastating animal that ever stuck his neck up into the sky is that he wants a stature and a destiny that is impossible for an animal; he wants an earth that is not an earth but a heaven, and the price for this kind of fantastic ambition is to make the earth an even more eager graveyard than it naturally is.

Ernest Becker, *Escape from Evil* (1975)

This is my dilemma. It is the dilemma of any genuine reformer or revolutionary. What is possible in man's evolution? What constitutes human potentiality and human nature itself? Can people ever really change society for the good of all its members and not just the privileged few? These to me are the vital questions that must be faced sooner or later. I am a reformer who believes that before anything worthwhile can be achieved for oppressed adults and children, the purpose, structures and mechanics of the dominant cultures in any society must be unmasked and shown for what they are.

There are layers of cultural conditioning and imprisonment within all human beings, most overwhelmingly among rejected and hurt children. Tom carries society's injunctions and prejudices as well as its vicious stigmatizations. He is, in many ways, his own brutalizer, accepting society's condemnations of his worth as a human being. He often says, 'I'm no good at anythin'.' 'I'm only shit', when he feels rejected and unable to cope.

The working class so often accepts the verdict of the respectable middle class on their own most spirited and rebellious children and supports the infliction of physical punishments in its local schools.

How can anyone affect and change these things?

Jonathan Kozol in *The Night is Dark and I am Far from Home* exposes, in the most stark and urgent style, the constructed, systematic brutalities of our age. He demands nothing short of committed action to radical change and upheaval, while making it clear that a serious personal price will have to be paid by genuine activists in their struggles.

He is right. Yet I am caught in a bind. The quote I have included in this diary entry has truth in it that I must acknowledge. People are paradoxical, insecure and at times vicious. But they are also capable of great heroic movements in the name of love, dignity and freedom. This contradiction leaves me feeling confused and impotent.

Ernest Becker says one must not be naïve about human nature and its possibilities and restraints. Jonathan Kozol argues that one must not be naïve about the man-made brutalities of our education and social system. If we aim to humanize our entire social structure, must we face up to our own human nature first?

This contradiction will probably stay with me all my life. There are four books that have deeply touched me in these areas. Apart from Becker's and Kozol's they are *Half the House* by Herbert Kohl and George Dennison's classic, *Lives of Children*.

Friday night

The local residents in Williamstown are agitating to close down the Coffee Shop. The battle to close it down has been waged over the last year by prominent churchgoers, members of the police force and parents from respectable backgrounds. As the Coffee Shop sits on church property and most of the adults who give up their Friday nights to work there are members of the church, pressures are being exerted on them. Many have started to back down and talk of the need for a quieter locality to be situated in a deserted area. Others are talking of turning the Coffee Shop into a type of exclusive club for less troubled kids.

It is only a matter of time before Rosemary and I will be forced out. We have tried on many occasions to convince the local minister and those on the controlling committee to allow the kids some say in the running of the place. When faced with repeated acts of vandalism, the church people have only seen the need to tighten control, not to create opportunities for any sharing of responsibilities between adults and kids. Until the sharing of collective responsibilities becomes a reality nothing will stem the frustrated acts of vandalism.

Saturday

I saw Lee Waxland today. There has been a gulf between us since our confrontation when Tom ran away to his place. I was glad to see him. He has so much potential and strength. Yet like many of the children and young adults I have worked with, he carries a series of traumas within him that are capable of exploding into erratic violence. His potential violence can be related to three or four specific traumatic moments in his childhood. These moments have been reinforced by the type of schooling and growing up he has gone through. If his natural leadership qualities could be channelled in a more positive way I'm sure he could become a good husband and father. But will he merely go on to perpetuate the brutalities of his upbringing on his own children?

The schools take little account of a child's passage into parenthood. Society itself ignores the growing up needs of its working-class children, if not all its middle-class ones as well.

Lee has developed his own capabilities as a future father and adult in the peer group structures. He will be an important adult in society if it will allow him to become one, and if he can somehow dislodge the traumas that seem to arrest his development.

Why don't the bastards who run this country shout it out for all to hear; the price of the majority group's affluence is the structured unemployment and soul murder of our kids, the expendable minority. Most of the kids who come to the Coffee Shop like Lee, Drew, Elaine and Judy are the expendable ones. Will Tom ever be able to work with any dignity in his lifetime? What reason is there in bringing children out of their traumatized states and helping them to establish their identity if all they face are lives of desolation?

December

Monday

We are nearly at the end of third term. Another hell of a weekend. On Saturday Tom woke up with two young cops standing over his bed. He was taken from his home and driven down to a deserted beach-front where one of the cops, after lighting a cigarette and staring out into the distance just long enough to unnerve Tom, asked him, 'Do you want us to take you down to the station and give you a belting in the backroom? Well if you don't, you're going to tell us all about . . .'

They threatened to take him straight out to Beltara if he didn't name certain kids involved in various petty crimes. He came back, according to his mother, white faced and shaking. When I got there he was withdrawn and terribly defensive.

Apparently about a month ago, Tom spent a weekend with Benny, Fred and Bernie, some of his old mates. He got high on a mixture of Southern Comfort and sleeping pills. A group broke into a local supermarket and took a few packets of chewing gum. Tom told me that he vaguely remembered being at old Sid's that night at the time of the supposed break-in but he didn't think he could prove this alibi. I too doubted this but said, 'All right, let's go down to Sid's and straighten this thing out.' He wasn't happy, just shrugged his shoulders and came. I went in to see Sid who did remember that Tom called in that night, but when I came out Tom was gone.

It was stupid of me, I should have stopped and talked over his fears about the police before we went to Sid's. Thinking back, I remember he was in a state of panic and fear. He was missing for the next twenty-six hours. He hid, trembling and desperate, away from everyone.

When I found him he was terribly shaken and I felt almost sick with relief. We had a quiet, intense session. I tried to cope with his fears. This had been the first time since I had become an authority figure in his life that the police had actually physically threatened him.

Next day I went and saw the chief detective to straighten things out. He was a narrow-minded yet friendly person, unlike so many of his colleagues. He gave me an undertaking that Tom would not be taken or interviewed without my presence in the future. Later, after a hectic, moving session with Tom about it all, I took him to see the chief detective. It was important to show him, face to face, that I would protect him, that he didn't have to be afraid in the presence of police, that the agreement was real. He felt the cops would pick him off the streets any time, regardless of what was said to me. Also it was vital for this policeman to see Tom and sense his distress and vulnerability in the context of my presence and care. I don't think the business will proceed any further.

Tuesday

I saw his teacher at The Annexe last night to discuss all that had happened. He was upset. 'Tom has been unbelievable since the catharsis you told me about. He's so different, I just can't believe it. His work is staggering. It will be tragic if this is upset now.'

Similarly, at home, he has been open, receptive, caring and helping.

This incident has convinced me how Tom has to be shown things, as if for the first time. Every one of his fears has to be brought to the surface and gone through; change has to be proved, bind for bind, hurt for hurt. His fears are so deep, so shattering. He has been almost broken by certain crushing past experiences. He has had absolutely no parental or adult protection. He can so easily screw up tight, and become rigid with fear. He has known no safe space to grow in, being in constant, trembling panic of looming, outside forces. Can he now have enough trust to progress, reassured by the events of the last few days?

Wednesday

Perhaps this time I have shown how some other options and actions are now open to him. He can recognize that we have done something meaningful, not just acted out of directionless rage. These children and their families have been deprived of the capacity to handle a situation so as to work it through to their own satisfaction. They have been robbed by a social structure that is geared ideologically to the submissiveness and vulnerability of its poorer economic groups.

I believe Tom now knows where he is, who he can really trust, and, most important, what is possible in a human situation when someone deeply cares and respects his being and existence.

Our relationship now has real significance. My caring has come alive to him in concrete ways. He can better understand the healing process in his own family. My love, care and anger are felt to be a natural, life-sustaining right. He now knows to give honesty in return. A hurt child is finding his own feet in the world. Life is taking on new meanings and possibilities. He now feels safe enough to grow in a more spontaneous way.

Monday

Our relationship has found its true centre. Over the weekend Tom ran hard against his own inner fears. He took a motor bike out for a ride, felt the power between his legs, smelt the dust and engine fumes, experienced the old magnetism of the chase, the hunt, the siege. He met some bikies, was tempted to run with them, somewhere, anywhere, off to unknown, unexplored territory.

I found him. We confronted each other and reached an agreement. It is Tom's right to expect to be prevented from riding bikes during the twelve months of the good behaviour bond. It is his right to be angry with me if I let him down.

'I'm all right as long as I know yuh care enough to help me. I don't care what the others say. If yuh say no, I know yuh'll stop me gettin' all tied up and runnin' off into trouble. I can't do it meself.'

This stage has only been reached after we have experienced the frustrations, let-downs, successes, traumas and testings; the relational stages and breakthroughs together. I believe the deprived, unhappy child needs continual guidance. This may encompass anything from support, care and love, to action, anger and enforced working-through therapy. But above all, it must be founded on mutual trust.

My relationship with Tom has sustained itself. It has been a labour of love and the commitment has been infused with a mutuality of respect and affection. The growing bond between us provides its own, at times, perverse momentum.

1977

February

This is a written account of a trip Tom and I took during February down the Murray River. I kept a diary record of my own, as with the rest of this book, but I also pieced together from our conversations during the trip a series of Tom's observations and feelings. As we worked our way down the river some of the most traumatic moments from his past came to light.

Tom's looking forward to the trip. He thinks about the fishing he'll do.

With sinkers yuh gotta have the right knack to put 'em on or else yuh lose 'em, the way we lost half a dozen the other night off the Pier. Just as well we learned how to tie those stones on. Only trouble is yuh need the right shape ones, the ones that worked real good the other night. Rosemary says a person better know 'bout all the stuff around him when he's out in nature or else he don't survive. Kayaks need the same type of thinkin' John tells me, yuh gotta patch up the holes and things with what yuh can find. He's helpin' me get an old kayak ready for our trip down the Murray. The glue we use smells like the stuff me dad mended shoes with. It hits yuh in the nose all strong, right between the eyes and leaves yuh all choked up with it — makes me feel real good and spunky.

Saturday

Jeez, I thought this was gonna be easy, but we've had a long trip up and now all there is is fuckin' water, reflectin' and burnin' yuh under the chin. Yuh have to think of bloody everythin', no one else out here to help. It burns yer 'ands, burns yer 'ead, makes yuh feel real sick. John keeps right on paddlin' 'cause he's done it before.

Them trees, John says they're river gums, fallin' right across the water, all grey, ghostly, like their twisted arms reach out for yuh. Yuh wanna get close to 'em and touch 'em and run yer 'ands along the top where there's all this peeled bark. It comes off like skin does when yuh've got sunburn bad. I got John to stop near one of 'em so I could feel it in me hands and it felt real good, kinda soft and clingin' to me.

Thinkin' about Duncan's trial for murder. He slit this taxi driver's throat. Me and John and Rosemary went to court; don't like the place, good to be between Rosemary and John. Poor Duncan standin' there alone; everybody just starin' at 'im up there, walls comin' in hard; wonder if he knows somebody still cares.

There's the king of the castle; who's the man under him? Then the next row, who's the man who keeps yellin'? John says he's the prosecutor; he keeps yellin', 'The defendant said he was gutless; he should have finished him more quickly,' not once, five times. Does he think we're deaf?

What are all them schoolgirls writin'? They don't understand. Keep lookin' at the judge, face made of old cardboard. Seems to think he's real good, says it's thanks to him the jury'll have a hot dinner. Speaks like we're shit. Great high roof reaches up, can't see what it's made of, stretches away from yuh, smooth shiny wood everywhere. People wear these grey, dirty wigs.

It's strange how yuh feel here, like everyone watches yuh real close and hard like yuh're on trial.

A doctor tells how the driver's throat got cut, real deep and long; went on and on 'bout how yuh'd stick a knife in so far. Made me feel real sick in the gut.

All them old ladies sit up in the jury. Yuh can just see what they think of Duncan, their minds all made up, plain as can be, he's just no good, yuh can just feel it. We're leavin' now. Rosemary doesn't feel too good. John's gone real white. Me, I seen it before when I was in Baltara, yuh're fucked and there ain't nothin' yuh can do 'bout it.

Up in them cliffs we used to stay. Yuh've gotta watch for snake holes me dad said, they sleep in the long grass in the hot sun and yuh can easy step on 'em. They get mean when they're woken. Their eyes are real beady, they stare yer out, all shiny black. I saw this dead snake lyin' in front of an old tree with millions of ants crawlin' all over it. Yuh couldn't see it for ants. Funny isn't it, the snake with all its poison being carried away by all them little ants? Me old man used to chuck out crusts from sandwiches and see how long it would take them to cart it all away. He made me mum mad not eatin' our crusts, just wastin' 'em on the ants.

The sun's in yer face, drives yuh nuts. It won't leave yuh alone, makes yuh feel all sick and wishin' yuh'd never come. Stop for a break and fall in the water. Feels shivery but it don't make no difference. It keeps comin' down, burnin' away until yuh think yer head's gonna burst, workin' away at yuh all the time, and yuh say to yerself all the time, it's gotta end sooner or later. The sun looks all white and bleary and the water's like a mirror. Yuh wish it was the surf with its foam all cool round yer body, not like this fuckin' cage. In the surf the waves are real big, ten, fifteen foot. Yet they're always smaller than yuh reckon. Walls of water sorta look down on yuh. Can yuh make it this time? Froth breakin', yer pulse beats loud, up yuh go, meetin' the sky, seein' the cliffs over the rocks. Can I make it? The frothy stuff surges about yuh. Shit scared, board gone, all tumblin', nose bubblin' full of water, sand and bottom, lungs burstin', struggle for surface. Is it worth it? Get yer board back and start it all again. Can't give in. John tells me to become part of the elements, move with the water, don't fight it, have to know the tides and currents, watch the swell, keep an eye on the sky, storms don't just happen. Later yuh walk along the beach, toes tickled by the sand, sun warms yer cold body. Funny, the different moods of the sun.

Saturday night

We sit and talk. Tom wants to show me something of the reality of his past.

'Payne got me into his office and said he was gonna give me six of the best for doin' somethin' to the toilets . . . I was in me shorts and he said he'd hit me on the legs if I didn't put me hands out both together like this . . . this was the year before yuh came. He stood by his desk with his strap in his hands goin' like this with it. I don't tell other people these things.

'He hit me four times right across the fingers on purpose. I don't want to talk 'bout it . . . He kept threatenin' me and sayin' he'd give me one more, one more. Me hands had marks all over 'em. I was gettin' funny in me head, like thinkin' 'bout jumpin' through his window and he kept goin', "One more, one more."

'I'd pull me hands back and I was cryin' and callin' him names and tellin' him to come and fight me out in the passage, and I finally went right off and started throwin' meself around and he got a bit worried and said, "Now Tom, don't get worked up. Wipe the tears away and sit down for a while." He was frightened of all the noise I was makin'. They always get yuh in the end, one way or the other, and yuh can't stand to think of what they did so yuh don't tell no one at all, just get by yerself and get all tight and wanna kill somebody

'. . . I never thought anyone could really help yuh with these things.'

Monday

One of them waterhens crosses in front of us with her babies, all in a row. The mother's in front. She turns sometimes to see if the little ones make it all right, glidin' right across the water, headin' for shelter, like me board headin' out towards the clear water on a big surfin' day. The hens move real fast like they know what they're doin'.

Mosquitoes drive yuh nuts when yuh wanna fish. They buzz and bite all the time. If yuh burn cow dung they leave yuh alone. Not many redfin this year, been ate out by European carp.

John's just about got the fire ready for tea. It glows bright, makes shadows across our sandbar. It's real nice, quiet with the cracklin' of the fire. I like lookin' up at the sky. It's black like velvet, twinklin' with lights. It makes yuh feel part of everythin'.

Me old man used to sit for hours on them river banks, fishin' and drinkin'. I'd sit with 'im and he'd tell me 'bout his truckin' times.

John wants me to come and get some tea and I'm thinkin' more about how me old man used to get real mean when me mum interrup'd his drinkin' and we had to leave the river.

Yuh know it's hard to hide things out here in the dark, things flood back and John just won't let me pass over 'em.

Monday night

We've had a hard, toiling day. Sheer heat. Tom's earlier journey on this river has come back to him. Something stark and real seeks expression in his every movement. We talk about his family's trips down here. He grows restless, animated, explosive.

'I wanna get out for a while.'

'No, sit and tell me what's worrying you, Tom.'

'Nah, let me go. I wanna get out.'

I playfully block his exit, though not *so* playfully. He stiffens, lashes out at me, connects with the tent poles and down we go under it all. He's fighting wildly against encagement and me striking out with mounting emotion.

'Fuck off! Let me out, let me out, I can't stand it!'

Somehow I grab him tight and throw the entangled tent off our heads and say, 'Tom tell what it is.'

'Nothin'.'

'Tell me what you see?'

We sit, my arms enclosing him for a long time. Slowly he starts rocking close in against me.

'I haven't told no one. It makes me feel sick inside and I wanna get tighter and tighter and just squeeze me hands together harder and harder. Yuh always push me one way or the other to talk about these things, makin' me so mad I wanna shut everythin' off. I can't with you. Yuh push hard until it all comes out and I say what's really gettin' to me and drivin' me nuts.

'Me dad promised me a horse. He worked where they keep the animals to slaughter 'em. It was to be my horse in a few days. We'd keep it, he said, and I could ride it around, I loved it, used to go and see it all the time, just to be around it. I was a real little kid. He killed it, my horse — well, I suppose it really wasn't mine. I wanted to believe what he'd said. He was my dad wasn't he? It was all hangin' up there, its guts out. He was takin' all its stomach out. It was upside down and still kickin' a bit. I can't stand talkin' 'bout it; blood and stuff dripped from its mouth . . . and one of its legs jerked out. I feel sick. He just killed it on me, after all he said, I ran out, wouldn't talk to no one. I used to sit by meself tryin' to hate him for what he done. I'd get real tight like I used to and wanna hit him or anyone who got in me way. Then I wanted to kill like he did to me horse. He didn't care.'

Tuesday

'Runnin', laughin', water around me. John tells jokes in the back, drinks one of the bottles of beer them nice people gave us back awhile. We flow with the windin' river. I direct us with me paddle. We've just been layin' back like this for miles, the boilin' sun on our faces and the water on our feet as they dangle both sides of the kayak. Birds sing up in the trees. Everythin's so clear and peaceful. We're glidin' with it, not sayin' a word.

Tuesday night

We're sitting around a campfire, drinking billy tea. Tom needs to talk.

'People just live in their own worlds, we all do . . . I know they aren't takin' no notice of what I'm sayin', as if I'm dead . . . then I go and sit by meself and tell meself "fuck 'em, who are they anyway?" But it still hurts a real lot. Sometimes I wanna smack one of 'em right in the face. I know I sometimes talk a bit, but that's because I never used to and now I really try to do the right things and it still doesn't make 'em respect me for what I am. Often I don't understand the way they talk to each other. They stick together and use their own words. People don't like anyone different from themselves.

'The Principal at the Tech. once told me I was an undesirable and not fit to be there and he's one of those part-ministers who looks down on people in churches, gets up and tells people how to live and everythin'. He made me feel, sort of unclean.

'When I was in the Home I couldn't understand why me mum left me there. I wouldn't talk to them psychologists who were tryin' to make me think I was crazy. I don't understand how yuh can love someone and just leave 'em alone. It's terrible the way they wreck yer trust with yer mum. I would sit by meself and not talk to anyone at all, just get tighter and tighter. I didn't cry as time went on, but I was really cryin' all the time on the inside.'

Wednesday

Me hands blister from splashin' water, gotta put thicker rope on the ends of me paddle to stop water runnin' back down it. It's real hard work holdin' a course against the wind. Yuh go off in the side currents and little eddies. Yuh strain every muscle. John pats me on the back, says, 'Give it a break for a while, take your mind into something else.'

What? Me back aches, got all these blisters. I know, I'll think 'bout that Saturday night at the You Yangs, cooler than here, yet I feel so warm and safe. Strange how the old mountain gum stands there on the cliff face after bushfires and all. Don't seem to be much for her roots to cling to as she reaches up to the sky. Wonder how long she's stood here. I wanna sit in her outstretched arms. They say yuh tell the age of a tree from the circles in its trunk. There's the big rock, it sits out all by itself, has a few boulders around as if nature built a stairway for a lookout. The rock's got little bubbles in it like the goose-bumps yuh get on yer skin on cold mornin's. On a fresh night like tonight the dew clings to the little bubbly parts.

I put me hand to me hair. I can feel the dampness there. The dark sky's around me close like a coat. Feel if I put out me hand I could pick the stars. Makes me think of stories John told me of the dreamtime: this land wasn't our land, it belonged to the Aboriginal people. They had beautiful stories, believed in their spirits. This place was their homeland, their tribal grounds. Where I stand on this rock I can feel 'em about me in the movin' of the shadows, the whisperin' of trees. Don't feel afraid, just part of their stories. Leaves yuh real warm inside. John says 'Come on Tom, back to work.' Sore, blisterin' hands, hard crosswind, choppy waves splashin' our food and clothes. Not far to go now, still got that warm feelin' . . .

Thursday

We're headin' back; lookin' for a ride, storm's comin' fast behind. John's real free, walks barefoot. Trucks pass, don't care much. Clear smell of things before a storm. Birds all twitter like they're warnin'. Winds blow in gusts. Everythin's covered with swirlin' dust. Have to shut yer eyes every now and then. Walkin's no trouble, free from that cage . . .

March

Monday

Back home the real struggle has started. Tom has yet to cope alone with everyday situations as he grows into adulthood. Together we have unearthed and worked through the major blocks in his past and tapped once hidden resources that make for survival. Now Tom must strike out on his own for self-realization.

I have learned a lot from our relationship and will continue to learn from the pressures that I know Tom will continue to put on me. I know now that most hurt, knotted children can only be helped by understanding the traumas in their lives. Once the worker discovers what these traumas are, progress can be made. It is important to understand that a child's behaviour is a direct result of them. The unknotting process, in fact the whole manner of stripping bare layers of hurt, follows on from this understanding. Without my confrontations with Tom and my growing knowledge of him little would have been achieved.

I have found that an approach that works with one child will not necessarily work with another. My approach with Tom has been to re-discover and work through his individual problems, and at the same time to struggle against our oppressive education and social system.

In my search for the 'therapy of disturbance' I soon realized that any child who has been helped to unearth his deepest traumas would then have to be taken naturally into a protective relationship and provided with the basics for survival and growth.

How does one provide the emotional support to back up the ongoing therapy? My own response, and this has upset many people, was actually to provide the psychological relationship myself while working closely with Tom's family. But what of the other hurt children who are equally in need? They too need the same continuing attention so that they can move forward. From my experience with this one child, I have come to understand the complexities and depths of many other children.

How can I put it? The Toms of this world will never really recover unless they have a combination of therapy and daily adult care in their lives. As difficult, and as unpopular as it sounds, society will have to construct, out of its own ashes if necessary, some type of therapeutic environment for these children. This will run smack into the present structures of our social and political system. It will run against our planned and deliberate manipulation of working-class children as the means of securing the success of the rich and the articulate. Some people will claim that it runs against human nature itself.

Those fighting alongside these children must develop a dynamic based on the realities of the children's needs and the realities of our post-industrial society. The struggle for the liberation of oppressed children involves the reconstruction of society itself.

Tuesday

There is one practical way in which humanitarian teachers can work for reform within the schools. It is the well-worn path of Thoreau, used by reformers like Gandhi and Martin Luther King. They can make the specific machinery of the system they oppose inoperative by blocking and disobeying its commands.

Take corporal punishment by strapping in the schools. The official policy and legalized sanctioning of corporal punishment, usually against the same few rebellious or unhappy children is an act of brutalization. The rules for the 'proper' infliction of corporal punishment on children are a mockery. Corporal punishment must be stopped. Without the introduction of some sort of legislation this can only be done by some teachers physically preventing other teachers from hitting children or, if this is impossible, by confiscating their straps and other instruments of torture. I remember the strange panic that followed my confiscation of a teacher's strap. Suddenly the school had a traitor in its midst. The teachers I had classified as authoritarian were on the defensive. They didn't feel as safe as before. If many teachers simply confiscated and destroyed every strap they saw lying around in schools, there would be pandemonium among their authoritarian colleagues. This has to be the first shot fired in the battle against corporal punishment and the abuse of children in schools.

Wednesday

Sunrise this morning started not only a new day for me but a new life. I have resigned under pressure from the Department and am about to go on the dole. I am free of the restraints of the education system. I will continue my work with hurt kids on my own terms. Yesterday one of the heads of Technical Education issued this ultimatum to me, 'You no longer have any prior commitments from us. You will work as we want you to, or you will never work with kids in our system.'

I left, saying, 'You haven't heard the last of me.'

And with this book I have kept my promise.

AUTHOR'S NOTE, 1982

In the last six years I have enlarged my understanding of many of the events recorded in this diary. I no longer rely so heavily on a restricted number of key terms such as 'trauma', 'lifescript', 'wholeness', 'self-realization', 'therapy' and so on. The past experiences of a damaged child would be understood in a far less restricted sense. Jules Henry is accurate in his statement that 'no single bit of behaviour can be considered alone; the significance of any event can be evaluated only as part of a configuration of events.' However, it would be an act of blind injustice to deny the hold and power of specific personal experiences in the lives of badly distressed human beings.

No one is more acutely aware of the limitations of publishing a personal, idiosyncratic version of daily actions and reflections than the author himself. What may be significant is the attempt to grasp the ongoing immediacy and physicality of actual human struggle. Also, I believe more strongly now that deeply troubled kids need to be confronted by the love and determination of insightful adult figures. I am convinced that both authoritarian and permissive methods of working with difficult and damaged kids have completely failed. We must struggle to find a practical hard-headed yet progressive alternative. As I wrote at the end of 1976, 'This may encompass anything from support, care and love, to action, anger and enforced working-through therapy. But above all it must be founded on mutual trust.'

John Embling
The Families in Distress Foundation
Melbourne, 1982